MEDITERRANEO
EDITIONS

Wild flowers of Crete

Text - Photographs
Vangelis Papiomytoglou

Translation
Jill Pittinger

Supervision of publication and maps
Mediterraneo Editions

This book is the result of numerous excursions into the Cretan countryside over the course of the last six years. All of the photographs were taken with care and respect for nature. Warm thanks are due to all the friends who accompanied me patiently to those places where the human presence still remains minimal.

ISBN 960-8227-77-1

VANGELIS PAPIOMYTOGLOU

Wild flowers of Crete

C O N T E N T S

CRETE, A LITTLE CONTINENT 6

FORMS, COLOURS, SCENTS 13

CUPRESSACEAE 20

DICOTYLEDONS 21

ACANTHACEAE 21

ACERACEAE 21

ANACARDIACEAE 22

APOCYNACEAE 22

ARALIACEAE 23

ARISTOLOCHIACEAE 23

ASCLEPIADACEAE 24

BERBERIDACEAE 25

BORAGINACEAE 25

CACTACEAE 32

CAMPANULACEAE 33

CAPPARACEAE 36

CAPRIFOLIACEAE 37

CARYOPHYLLACEAE 37

CHENOPODIACEAE 43

CISTACEAE 44

COMPOSITAE 46

CONVOLVULACEAE 66

CRASSULACEAE 69

CRUCIFERAE 72

CUCURBITACEAE 78

DIPSACACEAE 79

ERICACEAE 80

EUPHORBIACEAE 82

FAGACEAE 85

GENTIANACEAE 86

GERANIACEAE 87

GLOBULARIACEAE 88

GUTTIFERAE 89

LABIATAE 91

LAURACEAE 103

LEGUMINOSAE 103

LINACEAE 114

LORANTHACEAE 115

LYTHRACEAE	115	
MALVACEAE	116	
MORACEAE	117	
MYRTACEAE	118	
OXALIDACEAE	118	
PAEONIACEAE	118	
PAPAVERACEAE	119	
PHYTOLACCACEAE	121	
PLATANACEAE	121	
PLUMBAGINACEAE	122	
POLYGALACEAE	123	
PORTULACACEAE	123	
PRIMULACEAE	124	
PUNICACEAE	126	
RAFFLESIACEAE	126	
RANUNCULACEAE	126	
RESEDACEAE	130	
ROSACEAE	131	
RUBIACEAE	134	
RUTACEAE	135	

SAXIFRAGACEAE	136	
SCROPHULARIACEAE	136	
SOLANACEAE	140	
STYRACACEAE	141	
THYMELEACEAE	141	
ULMACEAE	143	
UMBELLIFERAE	143	
VALERIANACEAE	149	
VERBENACEAE	150	
VIOLACEAE	151	
MONOCOTYLEDONS	151	
AGAVACEAE	152	
AMARYLLIDACEAE	152	
ARACEAE	154	
DIOSCOREACEAE	156	
GRAMINEAE	157	
IRIDACEAE	157	
LILIACEAE	162	
ORCHIDACEAE	175	
PALMAE	193	

Chionodoxa nana

CRETE, A LITTLE CONTINENT

At the beginning of the Miocene, about 23 million years ago, what now constitutes the Aegean was an area of dry land which joined mainland Greece with Asia. This land, which has been named Aegaeis, also included the region in which Crete is situated. At length, 10-12 million years later, the waters of the Mediterranean began to flood Aegaeis, with the result that it was broken up into pieces and a group of islands was formed due to the sinking of large sections of land. These 'islands of Crete' remained as such through the Pliocene period (3.5 million years ago) and after continual changes, folding, subsidence, and uplifting of the land, Crete acquired the form which it has today, i.e. a continuous mountain chain with many gorges and plateaus.

The long interval during which Crete was isolated from the mainland – around 5 million years - together with the existence of high mountains which functioned as 'botanical islands' on the same island, explains the high degree of endemism amongst its flora (10%). On an east-west axis, Crete extends over a distance of 260 km, with a vertical axis fluctuating from 60 to 12 km. Its total surface area is 8,331 square kilometres, which makes it the fifth largest island in the Mediterranean. The predominant and most impressive aspect of Crete is its rapidly changing morphology, along with the altitude of the mountains. The mountain and alpine

The dwarf *Colchicum cretense* is endemic to Crete, i.e. it grows nowhere else. It is found in the three great mountain massifs of the island. The similar-looking *C. coustourieri* is an endemic plant with a very restricted occurrence, only growing on the Gaïdouronísi and Koufonísi islands of eastern Crete.

zone can be reached in a very short time from the coastal plain, since the three large mountain massifs, along with a number of smaller ones, cover more than half of the surface area of the island. These mostly limestone mountains are full of caves, gorges and streams which carry the products of erosion to the little plains and enclosed plateaus, producing a red soil which is rich in minerals and the remains of plant material.

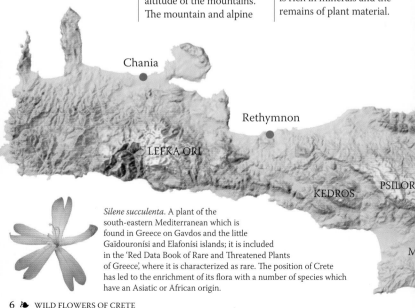

Chania

Rethymnon

LEFKA ORI

KEDROS

PSILOR

M

Silene succulenta. A plant of the south-eastern Mediterranean which is found in Greece on Gavdos and the little Gaïdouronísi and Elafonísi islands; it is included in the 'Red Data Book of Rare and Threatened Plants of Greece', where it is characterized as rare. The position of Crete has led to the enrichment of its flora with a number of species which have an Asiatic or African origin.

The denuded peaks of the White Mountains present the picture of an eerie and completely desertified region. The little endemic *Viola fragrans* and a multitude of crevasse plants, many of which are also endemic, grow amongst the stones. This richness rewards those who in the summer months visit this strange and at the same time bewitching region. The assistance of a guide well acquainted with the mountain tracks and the character of the terrain is, however, essential.

The relief of the terrain of Crete is characterized by the mountain massifs which cover the larger part of the island. These mountains constitute part of an arc which begins in the Dinaric Alps and runs through the mountain chains of Pindos, Agrafa, the Peloponnese, Crete, Karpathos and Rhodes, to end in Asia Minor. The huge massif of the White Mountains dominates in the west of Crete with more than 20 peaks exceeding 2000 metres in height; Pachnes reaches to 2452 m. The White Mountains

contain a large number of gorges, particularly those of Samaria, Imbros, Eligia, and Ayia Irini (among others), as well as the Omalos High Plateau which lies at the entrance to Samaria. Here, at Omalos, is the biotope of the endemic *Tulipa bakeri*. The Samaria Gorge is the most impressive of its kind in Europe and has been a protected National Park since 1962. Little forests predominate in the gorge, with funeral cypresses (*Cypressus sempervirens*),

The French explorer and botanist Pierre Belon (1517-1564) first described the *Paeonia clusii*, the endemic white peony of Crete; he found it on Ida, but it can no longer be seen there. Today, the only places where it is known to grow are in the White Mountains (in the Samaria Gorge and above Anopolis), and on Dikti.

Heraklion

Ay. Nikolaos

Sitia

DIKTI

THRIPTI

ASTEROUSSIA

Ierapetra

Calabrian pines (*Pinus brutia*), maples (*Acer sempervirens*) and Kermes oaks (*Quercus coccifera*). The park with its almost vertical slopes is a refuge for many rare, endemic plants and also for the unique Cretan wild goat or 'agrimi' (*Capra aegagrus cretica*). The gorges have been the scene of only little human activity over the years and constitute an important biotope for plants and animals. Nevertheless, the Samaria Gorge comes under great pressure during the summer months and for that reason strict rules apply to those who wish to pass through it.

The Idaian Cave on Psiloritis during the early days of May, when *Chionodoxa nana* springs out of the snow. Many endemic species are to be found in the surrounding area, while in the internal walls of the cave there is the rare and aptly named *Silene antri jovis* (silene of the cave of Zeus).

Samaria. The gorge, which has been characterized by UNESCO as a 'Biosphere Reserve', is home to more than 400 different species of plants, some of which are to be found nowhere else.

◀ A carpet of tulips (*T. bakeri*) on Omalos. If the field were to be cultivated, this picture would be lost forever.

The huge and compact bulk of Psiloritis (Idi) rises up almost in the middle of the island. Reaching to 2456 m, it is the highest mountain on Crete. At its heart there is the Nida High Plateau with the Idaian Cave where, according to mythology, Zeus was nurtured. The name of Idi comes from the Doric word '*Ida*' which means a forested mountain; this gives a picture of how it – and also the other mountains of Crete – would have appeared in antiquity. Today, the mountain once covered in forests

Crocus oreocreticus

exhibits the deep wounds which are the result of over-grazing, and in many places it is almost denuded. This, however, does not prevent a plethora of wild flowers from flowering amidst the phrygana, for example the supremely beautiful *Crocus oreocreticus* – the crocus of the Cretan mountains –

The endemic *Arum idaeum*. It takes its name from Idi but is found on all the mountains of the island.

Kermes oaks (*Q. coccifera*) and maples (*Acer sempervirens*) at Rouva. The forest cover of Crete amounts to less than 5% and is made up mainly of oaks and conifers. Otherwise, a large part of the island is covered by olive groves.

an endemic plant which flowers every autumn on all the Cretan mountains except for the White Mountains. Despite the downgrading, a glimmer of hope is provided by the Forest of Rouva on the south-eastern flank of Psiloritis. This unique oak forest, of which a section has already been fenced-off to protect it from grazing animals, constitutes a biotope for the endangered Cretan hooded cephalanthera (*Cephalanthera cucullata*).

In the east of the island, Mount Dikti with its plateaus rises to a height of 2150 m. The main plateau is that of Lasithi, which is a huge closed basin 12 km in length and 6 km wide; it is the largest on Crete and at one time several thousand windmills were to be found there. From the plateau, a track leads up to the Diktaian Cave where - according to tradition - Zeus was born. Further to the east there is Thripti (Afentis, 1476 m), a mountain with a great degree of endemism amongst the flora and thus of extreme botanical interest. Mount Kedros (1777 m) to the west of Psiloritis also presents great botanical interest with its multitude of orchid species, as does the Asteroussia range (Kofinas 1271 m) to the south-east of the Mesara Plain. *Scabioza minoana* ssp. *asterusica* grows on the slopes of Kofinas and is endemic to the mountain. The Mesara is the only large plain of Crete and with its thousands of hothouses produces vegetables all year round – the price, however, is the jarring sight of their torn plastic coverings. Nevertheless, the little hills in the villages around the Mesara abound with orchids and constitute a paradise for their devotees.

The Katharó mountain plateau on Dikti. Apart from the great Lasithi Plateau, there are a number of smaller ones, all of particular botanical interest.

Helichrysum doerfleri

The Bay of Mirabello from Thripti. The mountain is a real botanical paradise and is home to a number of endemic species with an extremely narrow distribution, such as *Ophrys thriptiensis* and *Helichrysum doerfleri*. A large part of the mountain is covered by Calabrian pine (*Pinus brutia*).

The coastline of Crete is indented like that of the rest of Greece and characterized both by beautiful sandy beaches as well as steep, rocky shores. Many beautiful species with particular preferences find a home here. Of these, the sea daffodil (*Pancratium maritimum*) - one of the most common - as well as *Androcymbium rechingeri* – one of the rarest – prefer sandy beaches. These biotopes are being subjected to increasing pressure, especially during the summer months; one such is Vai in the north-east of the island, which is the basic biotope for the endemic palm (*Phoenix theophrastii*). It has become such a tourist destination that it is really better avoided.

Century plant (*Agave americana*) on Imeri Gramvóusa, the little island opposite the enchanting beach of Bálos in the west of the peninsula of the same name. This species from Mexico, which was first brought to the Mediterranean area in 1600, dominates on the little island.

The four peninsulas and all the smaller islets which make up Crete are home to important biotopes for rare species of plants. The little Imeri islands and Agria Gramvousa, for example, are the biotope for two very rare species – a type of wild garlic (*Allium platakisii*), and a small daisy (*Anthemis glaberrima*).

For administrative purposes, Crete is divided into four Prefectures, those of Hania, Rethymnon, Heraklion and Lasithi. A dense road network traverses the island, which makes access to almost every part an easy matter. These roads often run between endless olive groves, which on Crete cover more than half of the area under cultivation. Olives and olive oil constitute a basic ingredient of the Cretan diet, a fact which explains the low percentage of cardiac disease among the island

According to mythology, Athena beat Poseidon in a contest to decide who would be the patron-protector of Athens by planting an olive tree; at the ancient Olympic Games the victors were awarded only an olive branch. The cultivation of this blessed tree began in the Minoan period and has continued unbroken to the present day, at the same time providing us with a mass of symbolism.

inhabitants.

Two basic elements of the Cretan landscape are also phrygana and Mediterranean maquis. The term 'phrygana' was first used by Theophrastus in order to describe small, tough-leaved, thorny bushes. Today, the term is used in a much more general way to describe downgraded, low scrub on stony, infertile soil. The essential oils, the thorns and also the form that these bushes take all combine to afford them protection from grazing animals and at the same time provide a haven for a number of herbaceous wild flowers which grow amongst them, in particular the orchids. Here – particularly in the spring and summer - the fragrances exuded are almost choking in their intensity, since the essential oils are diffused by the hot atmosphere. Such biotopes are to be found from sea level right up to the mountain zone. The Mediterranean maquis consists mainly of arbutus, oaks, and heathers, often covering large areas. Here, the foliage is sometimes so dense that it is impenetrable.

In spring, a multitude of herbaceous plants flower amidst the phrygana; predominant among them are the orchids.

FORMS COLOURS SCENTS

The infinite variety and multitude of colours, and often the fragrance of the flowers, make them very attractive but at the same time create problems of their classification, particularly for non-specialists.

Systematic botany divides the 'Plant Kingdom' into phyla. The plants which are presented here all belong to the angiosperms (ANGIOSPERMAE) with the exception of some conifers, which are gymnosperms (GYMNOSPERMAE). The phyla divide into classes, which in the case of the angiosperms are the monocotyledons or 'monocots' (monokotyledonae) and the dicotyledons or 'dicots' (DIKOTYLEDONAE). In general terms, every class divides into families which in turn divide into genera. Every genus is composed of species related to each other, with the name of each consisting of two components; the first of these identifies the genus and the second, the species. This system of taxonomic classification with its use of double Latin nomenclature was devised by the Swede CARL VON LINNÉ (LINNAEUS, 1707-1778), who revolutionised systematic botany with his work 'SYSTEMA NATURAE'. The Latin names constitute a bridge amongst scientific researchers and use a plethora of Greek words whose etymology - where practicable - accompanies the description of the species in this book. In the example, the taxonomic structure of two species is clearly shown. The letters which follow the name indicate the botanist who first described the plant. L. refers to LINNAEUS.

DICOTYLEDONS

The dicotyledons (DICOTYLEDONAE) constitute one of the two large classes of angiosperms. As is apparent from their name, they have two seed-leaves. The leaves of the dicotyledons are characterized by a network of veining, in contrast to monocotyledons which have parallel veining. The great majority of the flower-bearing plants, from the strange aristolochia to the common daisy, belong to the dicotyledons. The form and the fragrance of the flowers are both very important where the process of pollination is concerned. For example, aristolochia attracts flies with its unpleasant smell and temporarily traps them in its peculiar tube-like flower. The name Aristolochia derives from the Greek words ariston (meaning 'best') and lochia meaning 'birth', because the ancients believed that the plant aided the birth process. About 10 varieties are found in Greece, some of which are cultivated as decorative plants.

The genus Anchusa belongs to the BORAGINACEAE family; its flowers have five petals, usually blue and more rarely white or pink. Another member of the family is the genus Onosma, with its characteristic yellow, tube-like flowers. The campanulas

Anchusa azurea

THE PLANT KINGDOM

↓

ANGIOSPERMS

DICOTYLEDONS

↓

FAMILY COMPOSITAE

↓

GENUS *Anthemis*

↓

SPECIES *chia*

Anthemis chia L.

MONOCOTYLEDONS

↓

FAMILY ORCHIDACEAE

↓

GENUS *Ophrys*

↓

SPECIES *bombyliflora*

Ophrys bombyliflora Link

(CAMPANULACEAE), another large family, are thus named because their flowers resemble little bells. They are five-lobed, nearly always light blue or violet, and more rarely white.

By contrast, the wild pinks (*Dianthus*) of the CARYOPHYLLACEAE family were thus named by the ancient Greeks because the plant was dedicated to Zeus (dianthus = 'the flower of Zeus'). The silenes, which are represented on Crete by 30 species, belong to the same family.

The 'ladanies' (*Cistus*) are very beautiful evergreen shrubs which prefer sunny, dry locations. Very often – and particularly on hot days - whole slopes covered with cistus seem to breathe out their scent. The flowers, which resemble roses, have five white or pink

Campanula spatulata

Silene cretica

Cistus creticus

petals and numerous yellow stamens. These are aromatic plants, and from certain species ladanum is extracted, a gum which is secreted by the leaf glands and has pharmaceutical properties. According to Dioscurides, it was collected either from the hair of goats, to which it had adhered, or with leather strips, as was still the practice on Crete in 1700, at the time when Tournefort was on his travels. Four species are found in Greece, two with white and two with pink flowers.

The Compositae or Asteraceae constitute the

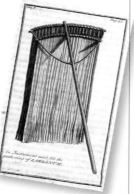

In Instrument used for the gathering of LADANUM.

largest family in the plant kingdom. Their 'flowers' (flower-bearing heads) are in reality made up of many smaller flowers which, in the daisies (*Anthemis, Chrysanthemum, Bellis* etc.) for example, are of two types – those

Chrysanthemum coronarium

Centaurea solstitialis

of the periphery (ray) and those of the disc.

The Centaurea also belong to this family. They are polymorphic, herbaceous or phrygano plants with flower-heads which consist of only tubular florets, those of the periphery being larger and sterile, and a very characteristic hypanth covered with spiny bracts. The genus took its name from the centaur Cheiron who tried, unsuccessfully, to heal his wounds with the 'great centaurion' which was possibly a species of centaurea. The amaranths (*Helichrysum*), cichory (*Cichorium*) and numerous other species, many of which bear spines, also belong to the same family.

The CRUCIFERAE, another large family, took their name from the shape of their flower which consists of 4 petals in the form of a cross.

Matthiola sinuata

The euphorbias (Euphorbia) or spurges as they are commonly known, belong to the family of the same name (EUPHORBIACEAE) and constitute a very large, polymorphic genus which includes both dwarf plants and small trees. All of the euphorbiae produce a milky juice which is an irritant and poisonous, as is the rest of the plant. Very typical are the flower spikes in which the male and female flowers are protected by two bracts which form a cup. The euphorbiae took their name from Euphorbus, a Greek physician of the 1st century AD who used their milky juice for medicinal purposes.

Euphorbia characias

Hypericum is a polymorphic genus which includes herbaceous plants, phrygana and shrubs. The flowers are often in a wave-like arrangement and normally have 5 sepals, 5 petals – usually yellow – and many stamens.

The hilanthi (LABIATAE) is a large family which includes phrygana or shrubs, usually aromatic due to the presence of glands on the leaves and stems which secrete essential oils. The pleasant aroma of the Greek countryside, especially during summer when the high temperatures assist in the sublimation of the oils, is due mainly to plants

Hypericum perforatum

Stachys cretica

such as sages, oregano and lavender, which are all members of this family. Two other anatomical characteristics of the labiatae are the generally almost quadrangular cross-section of the stem and the zygomorphic form of the flower, i.e. its symmetry on a vertical axis. The flowers have two lips - more rarely one - hence the Latin labiatae and Greek name hilanthí from the words meaning 'lip'.

The Psychanths (LEGUMINOSAE), that very large family which includes both small herbaceous plants and large trees, have certain particular characteristics which make the various species easily recognizable. The name of the family is from the Latin 'legumen' and naturally refers to the shape of the pericarp, which here is that of a bean. Notably, beans, lentils and lupins are all examples of members of this large family. The leaves are composite, i.e. made up of many smaller leaflets, although this is a characteristic also met in other plants.

PETAL

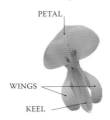

WINGS

KEEL

Their flowers are usually zygomorphic with 5 petals in a butterfly-like arrangement (hence the name 'Psychanths') consisting of a main, (standard) petal, wings and a keel, as shown in the picture.

The poppies, which in spring bathe the fields with their beautiful colour, are amongst the most loved wild flowers of the Greek countryside. Their leaves and stems are usually greygreen, while the flowers consist of two sepals which fall on flowering,

Papaver somniferum

and four petals which are normally red. A particular characteristic of poppies is the swollen capsule at the centre of the flower which contains the seeds, surrounded by many stamens. *Papaver somniferum* (Opium poppy) is the poppy from which opium is obtained through cuts in its spherical capsule. Cultivation is prohibited today.

Cyclamen are perennial herbaceous plants with a large tuber at the root from which the leaves and flowers grow on long stalks. The flowers are always white or pink, nodding, and have a very characteristic shape. The corolla is divided into five parts which are turned backwards in a spiral-like manner to cover the curved part of the flower-stalk.

Cyclamen graecum

The anemones (or wild poppies) are perennials, herbaceous plants with certain particular characteristics that make them easy to recognize and differentiate from the poppies and ranunculi, with many of which they are confused. The anemones do not have petals, while the perianth consists of the sepals which have taken the place of petals. The leaves grow at the base of the stem, except for three smaller leaves which are situated in a whorl a little way below the flower. The ranunculi belong

Anemone coronaria

Ranunculus asiaticus

to the same family as the anemones (RANUNCULACEAE).

Umbelliferae are herbaceous plants, distinguished by their inflorescence which takes the form of an umbel. The little flowers of the various genera, which normally have 5 petals, often resemble each other and this makes their differentiation difficult.

The monocotyledons (*Monocotyledonae*) constitute the second large class of angiosperms. As their name indicates, the seeds have one seed-leaf. The leaves of the monocotyledons are characterized by parallel veining, in contrast to those of the dicotyledons which have a network of veining. Relatively few families belong to this class; among them are many of the most beautiful wild flowers such as narcissi, crocuses, irises, colchicum, ornithogalum, tulips and orchids.

The narcissi grow from bulbs. Their flowers are very character-

Narcissus tazetta

istic; in the centre of the perianth, which is divided into 6 parts, there develops a cup-shaped corolla containing the stamens. The sternbergias, whose beautiful yellow flowers resemble those of the crocus, belong to the same family (AMARYLLIDACEAE).

The arums, and the Araceae in general, are easily recognised by the characteristic shape of their flower-head which consists of a tubular or funnel-shaped sheath (spathe) around an elongated spadix which bears tiny flowers, male above and female below. The leaves are usually dart-shaped on a long stalk. Pollination is carried out by insects which are attracted by the rank smell - which can be very pronounced – exuded by at least some of the Araceae. The attraction of pollinators by this method has given the name to this family, and to its largest species (Arum), which derives from the Greek word 'aroma'.

Arum creticum

The crocuses (Crocus) are very special wild flowers which bloom from the autumn to the spring. In particular the winter

6-part perianth

Anthers

Stigmas

Tube

Crocus cartwrightianus

crocus, which very often springs up out of the snow, offers pictures of unparalleled beauty in a season when most plants are dormant and preparing for spring. The crocuses have certain special characteristics, as for example the growth of flower and leaves directly from the bulb and the presence of three stigmas – the part of the plant which is harvested. Safran, as this important substance is called, consists of the stigmas of C. sativus, the cultivated crocus, which is grown in Greece around Kozani and yields a product of superb quality. The importance of the crocus even in antiquity is apparent from the famous wall-paintings at Knossos and on Santorini.

The irises take their name from the goddess

Gynandriris sisyrinchium

who carried messages between gods and mortals and used the rainbow as a bridge between the sky and the earth. They belong to the same family with crocus (IRIDACEAE). The beautiful flowers have some notable characteristics. The perianth consists of two types of 'petals'. The three external ones, which are larger, are spreading or drooping and in reality replace the calyx, since here there is no clear distinction between the calyx and corolla. The three internal ones are smaller, erect, and constitute real 'petals'. The style, which resembles the other parts of the perianth, is also divided into three parts and encloses the stamens. This multitude of components, together with their usually strong colouring, produces a flower which is very attractive both to humans and insects. The little bristles on the outer petals are also typical and are used to help support insects which visit the flower.

The wild onion (Allium, i.e. garlic in Latin) belongs to the same family (LILIACEAE) as colchicum, asphodel, ornithogalum and the tulips. These are plants which grow from bulbs with basal leaves and a stem that is usually long and, at its tip, has a head covered by a membranous spathe which splits open

Allium ampeloprasum

to reveal a globular umbel containing many flowers. The corolla is star-shaped or bell-shaped and divided into six parts (tepals).

Colchicum, these beautiful little pink lilies, grow from bulbs; they resemble the crocuses in appearance, although they are not connected to them in any way. In the colchicum, a tubular stem springs from the bulb and is surrounded by a spathe. At the tip of

Colchicum macrophyllum

the tube there develops the flower, with a perianth divided into 6 tepals. There are six stamens with anthers supported at the centre. The leaves usually appear before flowering. Most of the more than twenty varieties of colchicum which grow in Greece are autumn-flowering. All of the parts of the plant are poisonous, due to the presence of colchicine, a potent toxin. It was with this poison that Medea killed her children in Colchis; the plant was given the name colchicum.

The ornithogala (*Ornithogalum*) are el-

Ornithogalum nutans

and Crete. It is notable that of the 5 varieties which grow on Crete – if *Tulipa bakeri* is to be taken as a different species to *Tulipa saxatilis* – three of them are endemic.

The Fritillaria (Fritillaria), with their drooping heads and their distinctive colouring, could be characterized as poor relations of the tulips, but they nevertheless have a particular beauty of their own which stems from their fragile elegance. The shape of the flower and the square blazon patterns which they have on the exterior recall the *fritillus*, a cup used by the Romans to throw dice.

Finally, the large family of the orchids (ORCHIDACEAE) is that which has the most fanatical following. Around 65 species and subspecies of orchids are found on Crete, of which slightly fewer than half belong to the genus Ophrys. These very beautiful plants have some commmon characteristics. The flower, which is symmetrical on the axis (zygomorphic) consists of three sepals, two lateral and one central (dorsal). In front of the latter, two petals cover the reproductive organs of the plant, while a third petal, larger and

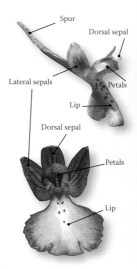

egant plants, growing from bulbs, which have white, star-like flowers. They retain their ancient Greek name of 'bird's milk' from órnis (bird) and gála (milk); the expression 'tou poulioú to gála' is used to refer to 'abundance' but here the name is probably connected with the white colour of the tepals, which in fact are usually green on the outside with a white border.

The most important representative of the lily family (LILIACEAE) is the tulip. Although Holland is considered by many to be the homeland of the tulip, in reality the eastern Mediterranean and Asia are the regions where self-sowing tulips are found; their bulbs were imported by the Dutch in the middle of the 16th century. In general, the tulips are plants which grow from bulbs and have a perianth divided into 6 parts (tepals) and 6 shorter stamens. More than 10 varieties of these beautiful wild flowers are found in Greece, most of them concentrated on Chios

Tulipa bakeri

Fritillaria graeca. This was discovered 60 years ago on the Rodopi Peninsula and has not been observed since then. The photograph was taken on Hymettos.

different to the others, extends forwards to form that which is designated as the lip. The latter, more or less, determines the appearance of the flower, since it may be entire or divided into lobes, and may or may not bear a pattern. At the base of the lip in some species there is the entrance to the spur which carries the nectar, in order to attract pollinators, while in other species the shapes of the lip are those which attract the insects, a technique which is used to a certain extent by the genus Ophrys. These little orchids, which are not by chance known as 'little bees' by the local people, are represented on Crete through 29 different species and subspecies. Of particular interest is the shape of the flower of this genus and the way in which insects are attracted for pollination. The flower consists of three sepals, two terminal and one central (dorsal) and three petals, of which the middle one is much larger, usually fleshy, and bears all the patterns and forms which make each species of Ophrys unique. At the base of the lip there is a stigmatic cavity and above it there hang two 'antenna' with sticky tips – the anthers. There is no spur, i.e. nectar-container, and what attracts insects is simply the appearance of the plant, which in each species resembles that of the female of a particular species of insect. This results in the landing of the respective male insect on the lip; in attempting to mate with what appears to be a female, it ruptures the anthers, which

adhere to its head. The insect carries them to the next flower, deposits them on the stigma and thus fertilization is accomplished. This 'sexual mimicry' sometimes confuses insects with the result that a multitude of hybrids has come into existence, making the already difficult process of indentification of these unique plants even more problematic.

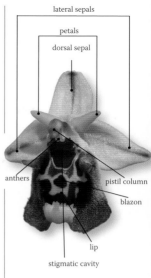

lateral sepals
petals
dorsal sepal
anthers
pistil column
blazon
lip
stigmatic cavity

EXPLANATION

CRETE
GREECE
NDEMIC

SCIENTIFIC NAME ↓

SYNONYM ↓

FAMILY ↓

● *Staehelina arborea* SCHREB. / syn. *Staehelina petiolata*   COMPOSITAE

Staehelina arborea

| 1 | 2 | 3 | 4 | 5 | 6 | 7 | 8 | 9 | 10 | 11 | 12 |

↑
COMMON NAME

FLOWERING PERIOD

SIZE ↓

DENSE DISTRIBUTION ↓

ABSENT ↓

 | 20-80cm ↑ |

DISTRIBUTION

ALTITUDE – CHARACTERISTICS

LOOSE DISTRIBUTION –

ZONES OF VEGETATION

COASTAL
0-20m

LOWLAND
20-300m

SEMI-MOUNTAINOUS
300-800m

MOUNTAIN
800-2000m

ALPINE
Above 2000m

SYMBOLS

HERBACEOUS

CLIMBING

PHRYGANO

BUSH, SCRUB

TREE

POISONOUS

MEDICINAL

EDIBLE

RARE

DECORATIVE

● *Cupressus sempervirens var. horizontalis* L.   CUPRESSACEAE

Cretan cypress

| 1 | 2 | 3 | 4 | 5 | 6 | 7 | 8 | 9 | 10 | 11 | 12 |

The cypress is perhaps the most characteristic of the trees of Crete. Despite the fact that *C. sempervirens var. horizontalis* constitutes one species along with the lofty-trunked cypress, it differs significantly in its appearance, developing an asymmetrical form and growing horizontally. A particular characteristic is its ability to produce stems from the trunk, which is unusual in conifers. It is said that the famous inverted columns in the Minoan palaces were made from the wood of the Cretan cypress.

 | 5-25m ↑ |

Juniperus oxycedrus L.   CUPRESSACEAE

Prickly juniper (cedar)

| 1 | 2 | 3 | 4 | 5 | 6 | 7 | 8 | 9 | 10 | 11 | 12 |

A tree or bush with leaves which grow in whorls of three, jagged and grey-green in colour with white linear markings to the right and left of their centre. The fruit are small and spherical, and turn red during their ripening period. They are consumed in some areas (*kedrókouka*). The subspecies *macrocarpa* grows on sandy areas near the sea, while the subspecies *oxycedrus* prefers mountainous localities and can be found up to the alpine zone, where it normally exists in shrub form.

 | 1-10m ↑ |

Juniperus phoenicea L.   CUPRESSACEAE

Phoenician juniper (shrub cypress)

| 1 | 2 | 3 | 4 | 5 | 6 | 7 | 8 | 9 | 10 | 11 | 12 |

In contrast to *J. oxycedrus*, the Phoenician juniper has dart-like leaves which, in the mature plant, are scale-like and resemble those of the cypress. The plant has stems branching off from the base and usually presents the picture of a bush, even though its height can sometimes exceed 4 metres. The spherical fruits are green and turn red during the ripening period. Normally found near the sea and in Mediterranean coppices.

|1-4m ↑ |

PINACEAE

`1 2 3 4 5 6 7 8 9 10 11 12`

Pinus brutia Ten.
Calabrian pine

The Calabrian pine can reach up to 30 metres in height; the pines of Samaria are very typical of this species. Another important population is found on Mount Thripti in eastern Crete. The resin which is exuded by the trunk of the tree gives a particular flavour to that purely Greek wine known as retsina. The forests of Calabrian pine extend up to 1200 metres above sea level and constitute a biotope for many species of orchid.

 | 5-30m ↑ |

ACANTHACEAE

`1 2 3 4 5 6 7 8 9 10 11 12`

Acanthus spinosus L.
Spiny acanthus

A perennial plant with opposite leaves, deeply divided and with spiny lobes and projecting ribs, concentrated at the base of the plant where they form a dense rosette with a diameter of almost 50cm. The flowers have a white lip, purple calyx, and thorny bracts, and form a dense spike at the top of an erect stem. Common in Crete, it prefers rocky and scrub localities, abandoned fields and olive groves.

 | 30-70cm ↑ |

ACERACEAE

`1 2 3 4 5 6 7 8 9 10 11 12`

Acer sempervirens L. / syn. *A. orientalis*, *A. creticum* ●
Acer sempervirens

This is the only maple which retains its leaves throughout the year – hence its name. The leaves are trilobate and leathery. The intense red colour is not due to the flowers but to the wide lobes of the fruit. The plant is found in the mountains in cypress and oak forests, up to the altitude of Mediterranean maquis.

 | 2-5m ↑ |

Pistacia lentiscus L.
Mastic tree, lentisc

ANACARDIACEAE

| 1 | 2 | 3 | 4 | 5 | 6 | 7 | 8 | 9 | 10 | 11 | 12 |

An evergreen, aromatic tree or bush with beautiful green foliage, very common in the Greek countryside. The leaves are composite with 2-5 pairs of elliptical leaflets, smooth on top and fuzzier on the underside. The plant is unisexual, bearing female flowers that are yellow and male flowers which are dark red. The fruits are small and spherical, red at the beginning and black when ripe.

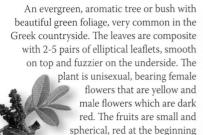

| 1-5m ↑ |

Pistacia terebinthus L.
Turpentine tree

ANACARDIACEAE

| 1 | 2 | 3 | 4 | 5 | 6 | 7 | 8 | 9 | 10 | 11 | 12 |

A deciduous bush with composite leaves which are smooth with 2-5 pairs of elliptical leaflets; in contrast to the similar-looking *P. lentiscus*, they have only one leaflet at the tip. The flowers are arranged in clusters on branches of the previous year's growth and the fruits are red, turning to brown when they are ripe. It is from this plant with a strong resinous scent that turpentine is collected, a resin with warming and other properties. The strange 'fruits' which often appear on the twigs are nothing more than galls, the products of small gnat-like insects.

| 2-5m ↑ |

Nerium oleander L.
Oleander

APOCYNACEAE

| 1 | 2 | 3 | 4 | 5 | 6 | 7 | 8 | 9 | 10 | 11 | 12 |

An impressive bush, and very decorative, for which reason it is often cultivated in lines along the edges of roads, presenting a unique sight during the flowering period at the beginning of summer. It has lanceolate, sharply-pointed leaves, in whorls of three, and large flowers, pink in colour, which grow in groups at the ends of the stems. Common in stream-beds and gorges. The cultivated varieties may have a white or red flower. The plant is so poisonous that even animals avoid it.

| 1-4m ↑ |

APOCYNACEAE

| 1 | 2 | 3 | 4 | 5 | 6 | 7 | 8 | 9 | 10 | 11 | 12 |

Vinca major
Greater periwinkle

A perennial plant, climbing or trailing, with large leaves, smooth and lanceolate, often heart-shaped at the base with a short stalk. The flower is blue-violet in colour, solitary, five-parted and 4-5cm in diameter, with a tube that is hairy on the inside and a long flower-stalk. Found in moist and shady locations. It is cultivated as an ornamental plant.

| 1-2m ↑ → | ⛰ 🌿 ⬛ 🌱

ARALIACEAE

| 1 | 2 | 3 | 4 | 5 | 6 | 7 | 8 | 9 | 10 | 11 | 12 |

Hedera helix L.
Ivy

Ivy was the favourite plant of Dionysos, and in all of the festivals held in his honour it was worn as a garland. This climbing plant with tendrils and beautiful leaves is very decorative and an ideal coverage for fences and walls. The flowers are small and develop in spherical umbels which later yield seeds in the form of small black berries. Found in hedges, amidst ruins and in thickets.

| 1-10m ↑ → | ⛰ 🌿 🌱

ARISTOLOCHIACEAE

| 1 | 2 | 3 | 4 | 5 | 6 | 7 | 8 | 9 | 10 | 11 | 12 |

Aristolochia cretica LAM. ●
Cretan Birthwort

This has an erect stem, often branching, with kidney-shaped leaves which are bilobate at the base. The flower is more than 6cm in width, brownish-yellow with a strongly curving tube and yellowish lip with many white hairs. It is endemic to Crete and Karpathos, relatively rare, and prefers rocky, shady places.

| 30-70cm ↑ | ⛰ ⚓ ◈ ⬛

Aristolochia sempervirens L.
Evergreen birthwort

1	2	3	4	5	6	7	8	9	10	11	12

A climbing plant with very long stems and heart-shaped leaves up to 6cm, smooth on the upper side. The flowers are up to 5cm on a long, thin stalk, brownish-red on the outside surface, and more yellow-ish on the inside with hairs at the mouth and a swollen base. Found in hedges, in thickets and in rocky locations. Very often cultivated as a decorative plant.

| 1-5m ↑ |

Cionura erecta (L.) Griseb.
Milkweed

1	2	3	4	5	6	7	8	9	10	11	12

A climbing, herbaceous plant with large, heart-shaped leaves, similar to ivy according to Dioscurides. White flowers, smooth, five-parted, in umbels. The fruits bear seeds with silky hairs similar to those of *Gomphocarpus fruticosus*. A fragrant but very poisonous plant, hence the popular name - 'death'. Found on steep rocky slopes, in stream-beds and on sandy beaches.

| 1-20m ↑ → |

Gomphocarpus fruticosus (L.) W.T. Aiton / syn. *Asclepias fruticosa*

Bristly-fruited silkweed

1	2	3	4	5	6	7	8	9	10	11	12

A tall plant with a much-branched stem and leaves up to 15cm in length, opposite, narrow and lanceolate with a strong central rib. White flowers, five-parted and occuring in umbels. The fruit is an egg-shaped, sharply-pointed capsule with hairy swellings. The seeds inside the capsule have a multitude of silky hairs which were used in the past as down. The plant has a North African origin, and is cultivated for decorative purposes; it is self-seeding in damp localities and road gullies.

| 1-2m ↑ |

BERBERIDACEAE

`1` `2` `3` **`4`** **`5`** **`6`** `7` `8` `9` `10` `11` `12`

Berberis cretica L. ●
Cretan barberry

A deciduous bush, consisting of many branches, bearing straight thorns; the leaves are unlobed and up to 2cm long. The small flowers are yellow and occur in clusters; the fruits are small, black berries. A plant which prefers rocky localities at higher altitudes, where it sometimes predominates and presents a beautiful picture during the flowering season.

| 30-100cm ↑ |

BORAGINACEAE

`1` **`2`** **`3`** **`4`** `5` `6` `7` `8` `9` **`10`** **`11`** **`12`**

Alkanna sieberi DC. ●
Alkanna sieberi

A small plant, erect or prostrate, and very hairy. The leaves are lanceolate, stalkless and covered with dense white hair. The flowers are rose-coloured or deep blue with a corolla double the length of the calyx. It is endemic to Crete and prefers sandy beaches, stony locations and phrygana near the sea.

| 10-30cm ↑ |

BORAGINACEAEA

`1` `2` **`3`** **`4`** **`5`** **`6`** `7` `8` `9` `10` `11` `12`

Alkanna tinctoria (L.) Tausch
Dyer's alkanet

A perennial, hairy plant with lanceolate leaves. Small flowers, light blue and in clusters. The root was used in the olden days as a dye, yielding a pinkish-red colour – hence the name of the plant. Found in barren and stony locations.

| 10-30cm ↑ → |

Anchusa aegyptiaca L.
Eastern anchusa

| 1 | 2 | 3 | 4 | 5 | 6 | 7 | 8 | 9 | 10 | 11 | 12 |

A perennial branching plant with lanceolate, fleshy leaves; the lower ones are stalked and the upper ones stalkless. The rough hairs and the white swollen flecks are very characteristic. The small, dead-white flowers grow in the leaf axils. The plant is found on a few rocky shores in southern and western Crete.

| 20cm ↑ | 🌿 ⛰

Anchusa azurea MILL. / syn. *Anchusa italica*
Large blue alkanet

| 1 | 2 | 3 | 4 | 5 | 6 | 7 | 8 | 9 | 10 | 11 | 12 |

The tallest of the anchusae, this is a beautiful plant with a densely branching, hairy stem. The leaves are lanceolate and entire; the lower leaves are large and stalked, the upper leaves are smaller and stalkless. The calyx has pointed tips and the flowers are blue or violet in colour, of a light shade in the centre and arranged in groups at the ends of the stems. Very common on roadsides and in abandoned fields.

| 50-120cm ↑ | ⛰ 🌿

● *Anchusa cespitosa* LAM.
Anchusa cespitosa

| 1 | 2 | 3 | 4 | 5 | 6 | 7 | 8 | 9 | 10 | 11 | 12 |

A plant with very short stems and elongated leaves, hairy and arranged in small rosettes. Endemic to the White Mountains of Crete, it is perhaps the most beautiful of the Greek ravine plants. The plant, which develops on the rocks and covers them with the dazzling blue of its flowers, makes an impressive picture and it is not by chance that shepherds name it for its colour – *blávi*, meaning 'blue'.

| 50cm ↑ | ⛰ 🌿 ◆

Anchusa undulata Lam. / syn. *Anchusa hybrida*

Undulate anchusa

| 1 | 2 | 3 | 4 | 5 | 6 | 7 | 8 | 9 | 10 | 11 | 12 |

An annual, hairy plant with leaves concentrated at the base, large, lanceolate and with an undulating lip, giving the plant its name.
Up to 5 flowers at the tips of the stems, small and funnel-like, blue or pink with sharply pointed petals. Found in fields, on slopes and roadsides.

| 20-40cm ↑ |

Anchusa variegata Lehm.

Variegated anchusa

| 1 | 2 | 3 | 4 | 5 | 6 | 7 | 8 | 9 | 10 | 11 | 12 |

As is apparent from its name, *A. variegata* is a plant with flowers that are a variety of colours. They are small and tubular, with five small, unequal white petals, with pink, violet or light blue spots. The calyx has five sharply-pointed lobes. A perennial, rather procumbent plant with leaves that have white stippling and are lanceolate, toothed, and bristly at the lip. Found in rocky locations, on slopes, and in ditches, often near the sea.

| 10-30cm → |

Borago officinalis L.

Borage

| 1 | 2 | 3 | 4 | 5 | 6 | 7 | 8 | 9 | 10 | 11 | 12 |

This is an annual plant, rich in potassium and other nitrous salts which give it a number of medicinal uses. It has a much-branching habit, and is hairy with large, stalked leaves that are ovate at the base; the upper ones are smaller and stalkless. Star-shaped flowers on long stalks, 'nodding' and blue in colour, and calyces with five narrow, lanceolate sepals which are shorter than the petals. Found in cultivated and fallow fields, phrygana etc.

| 30-70cm ↑ |

Cerinthe major L.
Honeywort

| 1 | 2 | 3 | 4 | 5 | 6 | 7 | 8 | 9 | 10 | 11 | 12 |

This is an annual. Its lower leaves are spatulate and stalked, the upper leaves are periblastic; all bear characteristic white stippling. The flowers are tubular and yellow, dark purple at the base and surrounded by leaf-like bracts, often dark in colour. Found in barren and damp fields.
C. retorta (Violet honeywort) is similar but a smaller plant; the lips of the corolla are violet in colour.

| 30-50cm ↑ |

Cynoglossum columnae Ten.
Houndstongue

| 1 | 2 | 3 | 4 | 5 | 6 | 7 | 8 | 9 | 10 | 11 | 12 |

An annual with large leaves, downy and stalked, the upper leaves stalkless. Small flowers, cup-shaped and brownish-red with five petals, covered by downy sepals of equal length. The name derives from the Greek words for 'dog' and 'tongue', and refers to the shape of the leaves. Found on the edges of fields, on slopes, and in stony locations.

| 25-45cm ↑ |

Cynoglossum creticum Mill.
Cretan houndstongue, Blue houndstongue

| 1 | 2 | 3 | 4 | 5 | 6 | 7 | 8 | 9 | 10 | 11 | 12 |

Similar to *C. columnae*, but with beautiful flowers of up to 12mm, pinkish-red or light blue at maturity, with darker veining in the same colours. The thorny fruits were at one time a favourite plaything with children, since they adhere easily to clothing. Found in rocky locations, olive groves and on the edges of fields.

| 20-60cm ↑ |

BORAGINACEAE

| 1 | 2 | 3 | 4 | 5 | 6 | 7 | 8 | 9 | 10 | 11 | 12 |

Cynoglossum sphacioticum Boiss. & Heldr. ●
Houndstongue

A perennial with elongated lanceolate leaves, covered with a dense, delicate white down. The colour of the flower ranges from violet to dark blue. The fruits have a sheath which is roughly haired and unlobed. The plant is endemic to the White Mountains, growing among the rocks at alpine altitudes.

| 5-10cm ↑ |

BORAGINACEAE

| 1 | 2 | 3 | 4 | 5 | 6 | 7 | 8 | 9 | 10 | 11 | 12 |

Echium angustifolium Mill.
Narrow-leaved bugloss

A hairy plant, much-branching and with narrow lanceolate leaves, from which it takes its name. The flower is usually purple or red with four projecting stamens. Found in rocky locations, on slopes, and often near the sea.

| 25-40cm ↑ |

BORAGINACEAE

| 1 | 2 | 3 | 4 | 5 | 6 | 7 | 8 | 9 | 10 | 11 | 12 |

Echium italicum L.
Pale bugloss

The name of this genus derives from the Greek word for 'viper' and refers to the shape of the fruit which resembles that of the head of the snake. *E. italicum* is a biennial, hairy, with a central stem which has many branches and gives it a very characteristic pyramidal shape. The leaves at the base are large, lanceolate, and concentrated in a rosette. The flowers are zygomorphic, in gentle shades of red and light blue, with the stamens projecting quite a way out of the corolla. Found in dry locations, uncultivated fields and on roadsides.

| 30-100cm ↑ |

Echium plantagineum L.

BORAGINACEAE

Purple viper's bugloss

| 1 | 2 | 3 | 4 | 5 | 6 | 7 | 8 | 9 | 10 | 11 | 12 |

A biennial plant, slightly downy. The leaves at the base are large with strong veining, in a rosette. A zygomorphic flower, red in colour at first and then gradually becoming mauve-blue. The calyx is short. Easily identified by its two protruding stamens. Normally found near the sea.

| 20-70cm ↑ |

Heliotropium europaeum L.

BORAGINACEAE

Heliotrope

| 1 | 2 | 3 | 4 | 5 | 6 | 7 | 8 | 9 | 10 | 11 | 12 |

A plant which is distinctive because of its curled, spiral flower-spikes. It has ovate leaves, lanceolate and downy, stalked and with marked veining, and white flowers with five petals which bloom from the bottom of the spike to the tip, the spiral of flowers opening slowly. The name comes from the Greek word for 'sun' and the verb meaning 'to change direction', since it is believed that the flowers turn towards the sun. Found in olive groves, uncultivated fields, and on roadsides.

| 5-40cm →↑ |

Lithodora hispidula (Sm.) Griseb.

BORAGINACEAE

Lithodora hispidula

| 1 | 2 | 3 | 4 | 5 | 6 | 7 | 8 | 9 | 10 | 11 | 12 |

A multi-stemmed phrygano plant, woody at the base with small, lanceolate, leathery leaves, with coarse hairs. Small flowers, five-lobed, bell-shaped, light blue or violet with a short, hairy calyx. It often grows amongst stones, a habit which gives its name from the Greek words for 'stone' and 'gift'. Found in ravines, rocky locations, and on vertical slopes.

| 10-40cm ↑ |

BORAGINACEAE

| 1 | 2 | 3 | 4 | 5 | 6 | 7 | 8 | 9 | 10 | 11 | 12 |

Lithospermum incrassatum Guss.

Gromwell

A rough-haired annual plant; the elongate-lanceolate leaves have strong fluting along their length. The small, funnel-shaped flowers are blue, on a thick stalk, a characteristic which gives the name to this species. The name of the genus derives from the Greek words '*líthos*' ('stone') and '*spérma*' ('seed') and refers to the irregular shape of the seeds. Found in localities in the mountain zone.

| 10-30cm ↑ |

BORAGINACEAE

| 1 | 2 | 3 | 4 | 5 | 6 | 7 | 8 | 9 | 10 | 11 | 12 |

syn. Paracaryum lithospermifolium

Mattiastrum lithospermifolium (Lam.) Brand.

Mattiastrum lithospermifolium

A plant almost identical with *C. sphacioticum*, both in respect of its leaves and its flowers. It is quite difficult to distinguish between the two, given their common biotope and flowering period. Nevertheless there is a characteristic difference in the appearance of the scales on the throat of the flower; in mattiastrum they are smooth, while in *cynoglossum* they are hairy. During the fruit-bearing period distinction is easier, since the fruits exhibit many differences. The subspecies *cariense* is found on Crete.

| 5-15cm ↑ |

BORAGINACEAE

| 1 | 2 | 3 | 4 | 5 | 6 | 7 | 8 | 9 | 10 | 11 | 12 |

Onosma erectum Sm.

Onosma erectum

A very beautiful perennial, with numerous erect stems and lanceolate, hairy leaves which are narrower. Yellow flowers, tubular and up to 4cm long, in dense, nodding tresses, with a sharply-lobed calyx which extends up to the middle of the tube. Found usually on slopes and in stony locations.

| 10-60cm ↑→ |

Onosma graecum Boiss.

Onosma graecum

| 1 | 2 | 3 | 4 | 5 | 6 | 7 | 8 | 9 | 10 | 11 | 12 |

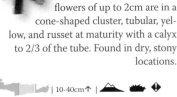

A biennial phrygano plant, very hairy. The rosette of oblong leaves develops during the first year, while in the second year the stem develops with lanceolate leaves. The flowers of up to 2cm are in a cone-shaped cluster, tubular, yellow, and russet at maturity with a calyx to 2/3 of the tube. Found in dry, stony locations.

| 10-40cm ↑ |

Procopiania cretica (Willd) Gusul. / syn. *Symphytum creticum*

Procopiana

| 1 | 2 | 3 | 4 | 5 | 6 | 7 | 8 | 9 | 10 | 11 | 12 |

A plant with rough hairs and large, dart-like leaves, heart-shaped with clear veining. The flower is very characteristic with five petals that are white, or more rarely light blue, long and thin, and turned backwards. The calyx has pointed lobes the length of the tube. Found on shady, rocky slopes.

| 20-50cm ↑ |

Opuntia ficus-indica Mill.

Prickly pear

| 1 | 2 | 3 | 4 | 5 | 6 | 7 | 8 | 9 | 10 | 11 | 12 |

Although a native of America, the prickly pear has acclimatized itself so well that it thrives in all the countries of the Mediterranean. It can take the form of a tree, although it more commonly occurs as a bush along hedgerows or fences. The stems consist of jointed, oval, fleshy segments, very prickly, and their length can reach to 40cm. The flowers are yellow. The fruit is cylindrical, red with countless tiny spines.

| 1-5m ↑ |

Campanula aizoon Boiss. & Heldr. ●
Campanula aizoon

1 2 3 4 5 6 7 8 9 10 11 12

One of the rarer campanulas with a restricted distribution on Parnassos, Gion, Helmo and in the White Mountains of Crete. It has a strong stem with a height often up to 30cm; the leaves are at the base, arranged in a rosette. The flowers are small, up to 1.5cm, dark bluish-violet, and the calyx has pointed lobes. It grows in rocky locations with a very small distribution and has been characterized as 'vulnerable'. The name comes from the Greek meaning 'that which lives forever'.

| 10-40cm ↑ |

Campanula cretica (A.DC.) D.Dietr. / syn. *Symphyamdra cretica* ●
Campanula cretica

1 2 3 4 5 6 7 8 9 10 11 12

This very beautiful and relatively rare plant produces large white or pink flowers which can be up to 5cm in length. The calyces have long, pointed lobes while the large, heart-shaped and slightly saw-toothed leaves have a long stalk and are concentrated at the base of the plant. It grows in varied biotopes, in a variety of sizes. Plants found at high altitudes are quite small.

| 20-50cm ↑ |

Campanula pelviformis Lam. ●
Campanula pelviformis

1 2 3 4 5 6 7 8 9 10 11 12

Endemic to the east of Crete, this plant has erect stems which are often woody, and hairy leaves, lanceolate, toothed and stalked at the base. The flowers are bluish-violet, up to 4cm, and take the form of a 'stamna' or water jar, divided at the top into lobes which fold backwards. The calyx has swellings and sharply-pointed lobes. Found on rocky slopes and in scrub.

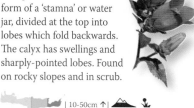

| 10-50cm ↑ |

● *Campanula saxatilis* ssp. *saxatilis* L.

Campanula saxatilis ssp. saxatilis

1 2 3 4 5 6 7 8 9 10 11 12

A perennial plant with many stems and smooth, spatulate leaves, slightly toothed. The flowers are tubular, blue-violet to white in colour and have a length of up to 3cm. As the name suggests, the plant prefers rocky slopes as well as old walls. Endemic to western Crete, it is relatively rare and usually found near the sea.

| 10 -30cm → |

● *Campanula spatulata* Sibth. & Sm.

Campanula spatulata

CAMPANULACEAE

1 2 3 4 5 6 7 8 9 10 11 12

This is one of the more frequently-occurring campanulae. The basal leaves are elliptical with a long, thin stalk. The flowers are on long stalks, funnel-shaped and divided to the middle, bluish-violet to white with dark veining. The calyx has straight lobes. Found in meadows, phrygana, clearings, and on roadsides.

| 20-50cm↑ |

● *Campanula tubulosa* Lam.

Campanula tubulosa

CAMPANULACEAE

1 2 3 4 5 6 7 8 9 10 11 12

This is a biennial plant, hairy and with the lower leaves stalked, ovate, and toothed; the upper leaves are stalkless. Tubular flowers, bluish-violet, more rarely white, up to 3cm. The calyx has lobes extending to the middle of the corolla, with two characteristic swellings at the base of each lobe. Endemic to western Crete, preferring rocky slopes.

| 20-40cm ↑ |

CAMPANULACEAE

| 1 | 2 | 3 | 4 | 5 | 6 | 7 | 8 | 9 | 10 | 11 | 12 |

Legousia falcata (Ten.) Janch.
Spicate Venus's Looking Glass

The wild violets belong to the same family as the campanulae, with flowers that open more widely than those of the latter. *L. falcata* has slightly toothed, stalked leaves, and a stem with a loose flower spike, violet in colour, on its upper half. The calyx has very thin lobes the same length as the corolla. Found in stony locations.

| 20-50cm ↑ |

CAMPANULACEAE

| 1 | 2 | 3 | 4 | 5 | 6 | 7 | 8 | 9 | 10 | 11 | 12 |

Legousia pentagonia (L.) Druce
Legousia pentagonia

An annual plant with many stems, its lower leaves inverted ovate in shape and stalked, the upper leaves stalkless. Corolla of up to 3cm and pentagonal in shape - hence its name. The calyx is downy with sharply-pointed lobes to 1/3 of the corolla. Found in stony locations and phrygana.

| 10-40cm ↑ |

CAMPANULACEAE

| 1 | 2 | 3 | 4 | 5 | 6 | 7 | 8 | 9 | 10 | 11 | 12 |

Legousia speculum-veneris (L.) Chaix
Large Venus's looking glass

Similar to the plant described above, but with flowers up to 2cm in size. The strange name of the species refers to the shell of the fruit which opens and scatters a myriad of glossy seeds like fragments of glass. This reminded the classically-educated Linaeus of the story of Erotas, son of Aphrodite, who found his mother's mirror in the hands of a shepherd and destroyed it to avert some tragedy.

| 10-40cm ↑ |

● *Petromarula pinnata* (L.) A.DC.
Rock lettuce

| 1 | 2 | 3 | 4 | 5 | 6 | 7 | 8 | 9 | 10 | 11 | 12 |

This endemic plant is of great importance, since it is the only representative of its genus. The deeply-divided, toothed leaves are concentrated at the base. The flowers have gentle shading from bluish violet to white with elongated petals turned backwards in large, cluster-like spikes. A very beautiful plant, which can be seen in flower on slopes and on old walls. Its name derives from the Greek words for *pétra* = rock and *maroúli* = lettuce.

| 20-70cm ↑ |

● *Solenopsis minuta* (L.) C. PRESL. / syn. *Laurentia gasparini*
Solenopsis minuta

| 1 | 2 | 3 | 4 | 5 | 6 | 7 | 8 | 9 | 10 | 11 | 12 |

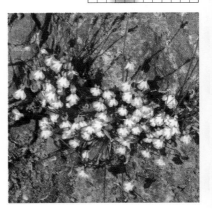

A small, elegant plant with spatulate, downy leaves. The flowers are light blue or violet on thin stalks, with a two-lipped corolla. The upper lip is smaller and bilobate, the lower one two-coloured with three lobes. The endemic subspecies *annua* is found on Crete, along with the non-endemic subspecies *minuta*, on rocky slopes and in damp locations.

| 5-20cm ↑ |

Capparis spinosa L.
Caper

| 1 | 2 | 3 | 4 | 5 | 6 | 7 | 8 | 9 | 10 | 11 | 12 |

A small, perennial, much-branched bush which prefers cliffs and crevices in walls. It produces many intertwining stems, and has leathery, ovate to almost round, smooth, stalked leaves. The flowers are large, on a long stalk, white or pink with 4 pink or green sepals and 4 white petals, which are larger. The stamens are red and characteristically there are many of them, longer than the petals; this gives the flower its particular appearance. The little buds of the caper are collected and preserved in salt, to be used as an accompaniment to salads.

| 30-100cm → |

CAPRIFOLIACEAE

| 1 | 2 | 3 | 4 | 5 | 6 | 7 | 8 | 9 | 10 | 11 | 12 |

Lonicera etrusca Santi
Honeysuckle

An evergreen bush, its stems much-branched and russet in colour, and grey-green leaves which are large (up to 8cm) and smooth. The upper leaves are fused and periblastic. The pleasantly-scented flowers occur in heads on a common stalk. Tubular corolla, two-lipped, white or pink, up to 5cm in diameter with long white stamens. Found in thickets, forests, and on rocky slopes.

| 1-3m ↑ |

CAPRIFOLIACEAE

| 1 | 2 | 3 | 4 | 5 | 6 | 7 | 8 | 9 | 10 | 11 | 12 |

Sambucus ebulus L.
Dwarf elder

A bush or tree with lanceolate, saw-edged leaves. The flowers are white, with 5 sharply-pointed petals, arranged in umbels. The fruits are black berries. This is a rank-smelling plant which spreads easily, creating large populations; it is toxic and has several uses in folk medicine. Found on roadsides, in ditches, and abandoned fields.

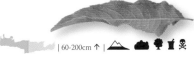

| 60-200cm ↑ |

CARYOPHYLLACEAE

| 1 | 2 | 3 | 4 | 5 | 6 | 7 | 8 | 9 | 10 | 11 | 12 |

Arenaria cretica Spreng.
Arenaria cretica

A perennial, hairy plant with spreading stems and fleshy, ovate leaves. The flowers are on long, erect stalks, white, with five petals and sepals half of the length of the petals. A very beautiful plant, forming white clumps in the crevices of rocks in the alpine zone.

| 10-20cm → |

Cerastium scaposum BOISS. & HELDR.
Cretan mouse-ear

CARYOPHYLLACEAE

| 1 | 2 | 3 | 4 | 5 | 6 | 7 | 8 | 9 | 10 | 11 | 12 |

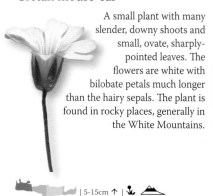

A small plant with many slender, downy shoots and small, ovate, sharply-pointed leaves. The flowers are white with bilobate petals much longer than the hairy sepals. The plant is found in rocky places, generally in the White Mountains.

| 5-15cm ↑ |

Dianthus juniperinus SM.
Dianthus juniperinus

CARYOPHYLLACEAE

| 1 | 2 | 3 | 4 | 5 | 6 | 7 | 8 | 9 | 10 | 11 | 12 |

A phrygano plant or small bush with many branches, woody, with narrow, pointed leaves, concentrated at the base of the flower-bearing stalks. The flowers have pink petals, toothed at the edges. Seven subspecies have been described, all endemic to Crete. Found on rocky slopes and steep cliffs.

| 30-80cm ↑ |

Dianthus sphacioticus BOISS. & HELDR.
Dianthus sphacioticus

CARYOPHYLLACEAE

| 1 | 2 | 3 | 4 | 5 | 6 | 7 | 8 | 9 | 10 | 11 | 12 |

This dainty endemic wild pink does not exceed 10cm in height and grows amongst stones in the alpine zone of the White Mountains. The flowers are solitary with an elongated calyx and sharply pointed lobes. The corolla is small, and pink in colour. The name of the genus means 'the plant of Zeus'.

| 5-10cm ↑ |

CARYOPHYLLACEAE

Minuartia verna (Boiss. & Spruner) Graebn.

Minuartia verna

| 1 | 2 | 3 | 4 | 5 | 6 | 7 | 8 | 9 | 10 | 11 | 12 |

These are small, grassy herbaceous plants which thrive normally at high altitudes. *M. verna* is much branched, very slightly downy to almost smooth, with small, straight, pointed leaves. The flowers are arranged in a loose spike with sharply-pointed petals, the same length as the sepals in the subspecies *attica* which is shown here. The minuartiae are a very beautiful species, with a considerable number of subspecies.

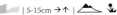

| 5-15cm →↑ |

CARYOPHYLLACEAE

Paronychia macrosepala Boiss.

Paronychia macrosepala

| 1 | 2 | 3 | 4 | 5 | 6 | 7 | 8 | 9 | 10 | 11 | 12 |

A small, grassy plant with small, opposite, lanceolate leaves. The little flowers have bracts that are very much larger, semi-transparent, silvery-yellow and membrane-like, which give the plant an ethereal appearance. The name derives from the Greek words *pará* and *nychi*, and describes the semi-transparent appearance of the bracts.

| 5-15cm → |

CARYOPHYLLACEAE

Petrorhagia dianthoides (Sm.) P.W. Ball & \Heywood ●

Petrorhagia dianthoides

| 1 | 2 | 3 | 4 | 5 | 6 | 7 | 8 | 9 | 10 | 11 | 12 |

A perennial plant with slender, erect stems and linear leaves. Up to 6 flowers in dense terminal inflorescences; the calyces have sharply pointed lobes. The petals are white with light pink veining, and untoothed. The plant is endemic to western Crete and found on rocky slopes and in gorges. *P. candica* is a more or less similar plant, also endemic.

| 20-40cm ↑ |

Petrorhagia velutina (Guss.) P.W.Ball & Heywood   CARYOPHYLLACEAE
Kohlrauschia

| 1 | 2 | 3 | 4 | 5 | 6 | 7 | 8 | 9 | 10 | 11 | 12 |

These plants resemble the wild pinks. *P. velutina* has a tall stem, downy, with small, linear leaves. The calyx is ovoid with flat scales and light pink petals, two-lobed with dark veining. Found in fallow fields and stony locations. The name is also of Greek origin, coming from the words *pétra* = rock, and *rígma* = crevice, which refer to the preferred biotope of some of the species.

| 10-50cm ↑ |

Silene behen L.
Silene behen

CARYOPHYLLACEAE

| 1 | 2 | 3 | 4 | 5 | 6 | 7 | 8 | 9 | 10 | 11 | 12 |

The silenes are represented on Crete by more than 30 species. They have a calyx with 5 teeth and 10 or more veins. The petals have a narrow 'fingernail' in the centre, forming a paracorolla. *S. behen* has a very characteristic calyx with pink veining – this makes it easily recognizable. The petals are whitish-pink. It is a rather rare plant, found in olive groves, gorges, stony locations and on seashores.

| 30cm ↑ |

Silene bellidifolia Juss. ex Jacq.
Silene bellidifolia

CARYOPHYLLACEAE

| 1 | 2 | 3 | 4 | 5 | 6 | 7 | 8 | 9 | 10 | 11 | 12 |

An erect, hairy plant with pink flowers. The calyx has typical parallel veining, green or dark red. The photograph clearly shows the paracorolla which is formed by the 'fingernail'. The petals of the silenes are very often rolled up spirally, towards the centre. Found in olive groves and abandoned fields.

| 20-40cm ↑ |

CARYOPHYLLACEAE

| 1 | 2 | 3 | 4 | 5 | 6 | 7 | 8 | 9 | 10 | 11 | 12 |

Silene colorata Poir.

Silene colorata

This plant prefers sandy beaches, where it often forms a beautiful pink mat. It has trailing or erect stems and small, lanceolate leaves. The flowers are on stalks and arranged in a loose spike. The calyx is cylindrical, swollen at the tip with russet-coloured stripes. The petals are pink, divided into two deep lobes. It is often to be found far away from the sea, on sandy soil.

 | 10-50cm → |

CARYOPHYLLACEAE

| 1 | 2 | 3 | 4 | 5 | 6 | 7 | 8 | 9 | 10 | 11 | 12 |

Silene cretica L.

Silene cretica

A delicate, slightly-branched annual. The lower leaves are elongated and inverted ovate in shape, the upper leaves are narrow and pointed. The calyx is smooth, narrower at the lips with green stripes. The petals are pink and divided into two lobes. Found in olive groves, uncultivated fields, and stony locations.

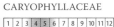 | 10-50cm ↑ |

CARYOPHYLLACEAE

| 1 | 2 | 3 | 4 | 5 | 6 | 7 | 8 | 9 | 10 | 11 | 12 |

Silene dichotoma Ehrh.

Forked catchfly

This plant has slightly downy stems which branch as if they have been bissected – hence the name. The upper leaves are lanceolate, the lower ones inverse-ovate. The calyx is hairy and has 10 veins. The petals are white and notched. The subspecies *racemosa* is met on Crete. The plant is found on slopes, roadsides and in fields.

 | 20-50cm ↑ |

Silene gallica L.
Small-flowered catchfly

| 1 | 2 | 3 | 4 | 5 | 6 | 7 | 8 | 9 | 10 | 11 | 12 |

An annual, downy plant, with slightly branching stems and opposite leaves; the upper ones are oblong, the lower ones inverted ovate in shape. The flowers are arranged in a loose spike with an ovoid calyx, narrow at the lip, very hairy with russet-coloured stripes. The petals are pink or more rarely white, and entire. Found in rocky locations, in fields and on roadsides.

| 20-50cm ↑ |

Silene sedoides Poir.
Silene sedoides

| 1 | 2 | 3 | 4 | 5 | 6 | 7 | 8 | 9 | 10 | 11 | 12 |

This tiny silene does not exceed 10cm in height and is easily distinguished by its fleshy leaves, which are similar to those of *Sedum*. It is a branching plant, hairy and with an elongated calyx and pink, slightly bilobate petals. Found in stony places near the sea.

 | 5-20cm ↑ |

Silene succulenta Forsk.
Silene succulenta

| 1 | 2 | 3 | 4 | 5 | 6 | 7 | 8 | 9 | 10 | 11 | 12 |

A hairy, sticky plant with inverse-lanceolate (oblong-lanceolate) fleshy leaves. The calyx is swollen with parallel veins and white or pink petals. The subspecies *succulenta*, which has an African origin, is found on Crete. It can be seen on the sandy beaches of Elafonísi, on Gavdos Island and on Gaïdouronísi. It has been characterized as rare.

 | 10-30cm ↑ → |

CARYOPHYLLACEAE

| 1 | 2 | 3 | 4 | 5 | 6 | 7 | 8 | 9 | 10 | 11 | 12 |

Silene variegata (Desf.) Boiss. & Heldr. ●
Silene variegata

A small plant, endemic to Crete. The leaves are grey-green, ovate, sharply-pointed and fleshy. The flowers have a cylindrical-ovoid calyx with brownish-pink veining. The petals are narrow, notched, and pink in colour. Found in stony locations at alpine altitudes and in the three mountain massifs of the island.

| 5-10cm ↑ |

CARYOPHYLLACEAE

| 1 | 2 | 3 | 4 | 5 | 6 | 7 | 8 | 9 | 10 | 11 | 12 |

Silene vulgaris (Moench) Garcke
Bladder campion

The most common of all the silenes, this is a perennial plant, smooth and much-branched, with stalked leaves which are lanceolate and up to 6cm; the upper leaves are stalkless. The calyx is light-coloured, beige or greenish, ovoid or almost spherical, with many veins and a mosaic-like blazon. The petals are white, two-lobed and fall easily, while the calyx remains. Found in uncultivated fields, on roadsides, and on slopes.

| 50-100cm ↑ → |

CHENOPODIACEAE

| 1 | 2 | 3 | 4 | 5 | 6 | 7 | 8 | 9 | 10 | 11 | 12 |

Salsola kali L.
Prickly saltwort

A shrub or phrygana plant with branching stems and fleshy, spine-tipped leaves. The flowers are small, yellowish-green and axillary. The plant is rich in nitric salts, and for this reason was used in the past to produce caustic soda, as was the similar *Salsola soda*. Found in coastal locations.

| 40-60cm ↑ |

Cistus creticus L. / syn. *Cistus incanus ssp. creticus*

CISTACEAE

Cistus creticus

| 1 | 2 | 3 | 4 | 5 | 6 | 7 | 8 | 9 | 10 | 11 | 12 |

This is the cistus from which gum ladanum was at one time collected. It is a shrub which produces many branches with short, white, sticky hairs and stalked leaves, opposite and gland-bearing, undulating at the edges. It has flowers of up to 6cm with short sepals and pink petals of a particular shape which gives a rather untidy appearance. It is often found in large populations on stony slopes and in thickets.

| 50-100cm ↑ →

Cistus parviflorus Lamk.

CISTACEAE

Small-flowered cistus

| 1 | 2 | 3 | 4 | 5 | 6 | 7 | 8 | 9 | 10 | 11 | 12 |

A much-branched shrub or phrygano plant with characteristic silver-green foliage, generally smaller and with a smaller distribution than *C. creticus*. The flowers do not exceed 3cm in diameter, and grow up to 6 together in umbels. The leaves are slightly downy, and billowy. Found in phrygana, thickets and pine forests.

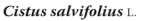 | 40-70cm ↑ →

Cistus salvifolius L.

CISTACEAE

Sage-leaved cistus

| 1 | 2 | 3 | 4 | 5 | 6 | 7 | 8 | 9 | 10 | 11 | 12 |

This is a hairy shrub with leaves which in contrast to the other cistus shrubs are non-sticky but resemble those of the sage - hence its name. The flowers are white on long stalks with a diameter of up to 5cm; sometimes there are so many of them that they almost cover the plant. Found in phrygana and thickets.

 | 30-90cm ↑ →

CISTACEAE

1 2 3 4 5 6 7 8 9 10 11 12

Fumana arabica (L.) Spach
Arabian fumana

A plant with long, branching, slender stems and lanceolate, alternate leaves. The flowers, which are yellow or have a slightly orange tinge, have a diameter of 2-2.5cm, with drooping petals. Found in phrygana and thickets, often lost amongst other plants.

| 20-50cm ↑ |

CISTACEAE

1 2 3 4 5 6 7 8 9 10 11 12

Fumana paphlagonica ssp. *alpina* Bornm. & Janch.
Fumana paphlagonica ssp. alpina

A dwarf plant with creeping, woody stems and linear leaves. The flowers have a diameter of 1.5-2cm, and are yellow. Found in stony places and in crevices in the alpine zone of the White Mountains, flowering in the summer.

| 5-15cm ↑ → |

CISTACEAE

1 2 3 4 5 6 7 8 9 10 11 12

Fumana thymifolia (L.) Spach
Thyme-leaved fumana

A small phrygano plant with many downy stems and small, lanceolate, opposite leaves which have lateral leaflets. The flowers are yellow, arranged in a small raceme, with a diameter not exceeding 1cm. Found in phrygana, thickets and stony locations.

| 10-30cm ↑ |

Helianthemum hymettium Boiss. & Heldr.
Helianthemum hymettium

CISTACEAE

| 1 | 2 | 3 | 4 | 5 | 6 | 7 | 8 | 9 | 10 | 11 | 12 |

The helianthema are little plants which belong to the same family as the cistus shrubs and have flowers more or less resembling them but smaller, usually yellow and more rarely white or pink. *H. hymettium* is a small, hairy, much-branched and trailing phrygano plant with opposite leaves that are ovate-lanceolate in shape and very hairy. The flowers are yellow and stalked, with a diameter that does not exceed 1cm. Found in rocky, mountainous locations.

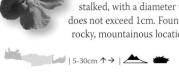

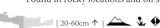 | 5-30cm ↑ →

Tuberaria guttata (L.) Fourr.
Annual or spotted rockrose

CISTACEAE

| 1 | 2 | 3 | 4 | 5 | 6 | 7 | 8 | 9 | 10 | 11 | 12 |

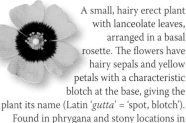

A small, hairy erect plant with lanceolate leaves, arranged in a basal rosette. The flowers have hairy sepals and yellow petals with a characteristic blotch at the base, giving the plant its name (Latin '*gutta*' = 'spot, blotch'). Found in phrygana and stony locations in western Crete.

 | 5-30cm ↑

Achillea cretica L.
Cretan yarrow

COMPOSITAE

| 1 | 2 | 3 | 4 | 5 | 6 | 7 | 8 | 9 | 10 | 11 | 12 |

More than 20 varieties of these very decorative plants are found in Greece which, because they are considered to have haemostatic (styptic) properties, bear the name of the Homeric hero Achilles who according to mythology gave the plant to his soldiers so that they could staunch their wounds. *A. cretica* is an elegant plant with many stems and elongated, wing-like leaves. The flowers are white and form an umbel. Found in rocky locations and on slopes.

| 20-60cm ↑

Anthemis chia L.
Greek chamomile

This little daisy is the most common in Greece and embellishes the fields in spring with its whitish-yellow colours. It has deeply-divided leaves, smooth or slightly downy. The flower-heads are on long stalks and up to 4cm in diameter, with the peripheral flowers white, tongue-like and with three little lobes at the tip. The central florets are all of the same height, yellow, and form a disc. Found in fields, olive groves, and on roadsides.

| 20-60cm ↑ | 🏔 🌊

Anthemis filicaulis BOISS & HELDR. ●
Anthemis filicaulis

This little daisy is endemic to north-eastern Crete. It has very thin, almost thread-like stems – a characteristic which gives it its name. The leaves are deeply divided and fleshy. The flower-bearing heads have 5-8 white, tongue-like peripheral florets. The disc is yellow. Found amidst coastal rocks.

| 10-30cm ↑ | 🏔

Anthemis rigida (SM.) BOISS. & HELDR.
Rayless chamomile

A small plant with spreading stems and deeply-divided leaves, which are slightly fleshy. The flower-heads are small, up to 1cm, with yellow florets. The peripheral florets are nearly always absent. Found in sandy and stony locations near the sea.

| 5-10cm → | 🏔 🌊

Aster creticus (Gand.) Rech.
Aster creticus

COMPOSITAE

| 1 | 2 | 3 | 4 | 5 | 6 | 7 | 8 | 9 | 10 | 11 | 12 |

A perennial with slender, erect stems. The leaves are elongated and lanceolate, alternate along the whole length of the stem. The flower-bearing heads are in dense terminal corymbs with very characteristic irregular florets in a variety of colours. The plant, which is endemic to the south-east Aegean, flowers in the autumn and is found in eastern Crete.

| 40cm ↑ |

Aster tripolium L.
Sea aster

COMPOSITAE

| 1 | 2 | 3 | 4 | 5 | 6 | 7 | 8 | 9 | 10 | 11 | 12 |

An erect plant, smooth and very branching with slender stems and oblong-lanceolate leaves, slightly fleshy. The flower-heads have elongated peripheral florets, light blue or violet and up to 2cm in length. The disc florets are yellow. A beautiful plant, often occurring in clumps; it prefers damp coastal locations and lagoons, flowering in the autumn.

| 20-60cm ↑ |

Atractylis gummifera L. / syn. *Carlina gummifera*
Pine thistle

COMPOSITAE

| 1 | 2 | 3 | 4 | 5 | 6 | 7 | 8 | 9 | 10 | 11 | 12 |

A perennial plant with a very short stem and leaves in a flattened rosette, oblong and deeply-divided with spiny lobes. At the centre of the rosette there develops a single flower-bearing head with a diameter of up to 6cm; it has lanceolate thorny bracts, those in the interior alternate with violet shading. The florets are numerous, pink, and remain for some time after the leaves have shrivelled. The plant is toxic, and used in folk medicine. In times past, children used the white substance that was exuded by the plant as a form of mastic or chewing gum. Found in barren, stony locations.

| 20-40 → |

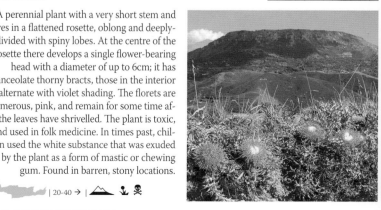

COMPOSITAE

| 1 | 2 | 3 | 4 | 5 | 6 | 7 | 8 | 9 | 10 | 11 | 12 |

Bellis longifolia Boiss. & Heldr. ●
Bellis longifolia

This little bellis is distinguished by its elongated saw-edged leaves which are concentrated in a basal rosette. The flowers resemble those of the other species of bellis and have a diameter of up to 2.5cm. The plant is endemic to Crete and found in the great mountain massifs of the island, at high altitudes.

| 10-20cm ↑ |

COMPOSITAE

| 1 | 2 | 3 | 4 | 5 | 6 | 7 | 8 | 9 | 10 | 11 | 12 |

Bellis perennis L.
Daisy

These small daisies are amongst the first to flower in winter. The plant is a perennial with ovate leaves, slightly toothed and stalked. The flower-bearing heads are up to 3cm in diameter with a long stalk that is bare or only lightly downy. The peripheral florets are lanceolate, and white with reddish 'brush-strokes' on the underside. The disc florets are yellow. Found in cool locations, fields and on roadsides.

| 10-30 ↑ |

COMPOSITAE

| 1 | 2 | 3 | 4 | 5 | 6 | 7 | 8 | 9 | 10 | 11 | 12 |

Bellis sylvestris Cyr.
Southern daisy

The fact that this plant begins to flower from autumn onwards when no other daisy is yet im bloom, and has elongated lanceolate leaves, makes *B. sylverstris* easily recognisable. The flower-bearing heads grow on very long stalks, have a diameter of up to 4cm and resemble those of the other varieties of *bellis*. Found in fields, meadows, and olive groves.

| 10-30cm ↑ |

Calendula arvensis L.
Field marigold

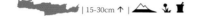

This little calendula does not exceed 30cm in height. It has lanceolate leaves that are often slightly toothed, the lower leaves stalked. The flower-heads are up to 2cm and all the florets are orange-coloured. The name derives from the Latin *Calendae* (calendar) and refers to the long period of flowering of these plants. In former times, the tongue-like florets of the calendula were used to adulterate saffron.

| 15-30cm ↑ |

● *Carlina corymbosa* **ssp. *curetum*** (Boiss.) Nyman   COMPOSITAE
Flat-topped carline thistle

The carlinae are thorny plants which took their name from Charlemagne, since he was believed to have used some of them to cure his army of the plague. *C. corymbosa* is a perennial with very spiny leaves and flower-heads up to 3cm, helmet-like, with yellow florets and leaf-   like bracts of brownish-yellow. Found in dry, infertile locations.

| 40-60cm ↑ |

Carthamus lanatus **ssp. *baeticus*** Nyman   COMPOSITAE
Carthamus lanatus ssp. baeticus

An annual thistle, much-branching and with deeply-divided leaves and lobes which terminate in strong thorns. The flower-heads are surrounded by spiny bracts which resemble the leaves and covered with dense woolly down. The florets are tubular and yellow. Found in barren locations. *Carthamus dentatus* ssp. *ruber* is similar, with pink flowers.

| 30-50cm ↑ |

COMPOSITAE

| 1 | 2 | 3 | 4 | 5 | 6 | 7 | 8 | 9 | 10 | 11 | 12 |

Centaurea calcitrapa L.
Red star thistle

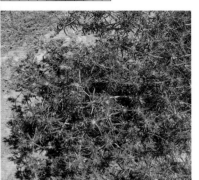

A biennial plant with many branches and deeply-divided, lanceolate leaves, the lower ones stalked and the upper ones narrower and stalkless. The flower-head has pink florets and a hypanth with fluted bracts, spiny and with the central spine very large and off-white in colour. Found on roadsides and on the perimeters of fields. Used in folk medicine as a febrifuge and tonic.

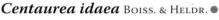 | 20-100cm ↑ |

COMPOSITAE

| 1 | 2 | 3 | 4 | 5 | 6 | 7 | 8 | 9 | 10 | 11 | 12 |

Centaurea idaea Boiss. & Heldr. ●
Centaurea idaea

A biennial plant with many winged stems and downy leaves arranged in a rosette, the lower ones deeply divided and the upper ones entire. The flower-head is hairy with yellow florets, and the hypanth has bracts that are yellowish and spiny, the largest spine up to 3cm in length. Endemic to Crete, the plant is common in stony locations at mountain altitudes.

 | 20-40cm ↑ |

COMPOSITAE

| 1 | 2 | 3 | 4 | 5 | 6 | 7 | 8 | 9 | 10 | 11 | 12 |

Centaurea raphanina ssp. *raphanina* ●
Centaurea raphanina

A perennial plant without a stem; it has smooth leaves, wing-lobed, in a prostrate rosette. The rhizome is tuberous and resembles a radish - hence its name. There are 2-4 flower-heads, pink and stalkless. The hypanth has eyelash-like bracts and a spine which is slightly larger. Found in stony places, on slopes, and in phrygana.

 | 10-15cm → |

Centaurea spinosa L.

Centaurea spinosa

| 1 | 2 | 3 | 4 | 5 | 6 | 7 | 8 | 9 | 10 | 11 | 12 |

C. spinosa is one of the most impressive of the centaureae. It has a much-branched stem and is extremely spiny. It has solitary flower-heads with whitish-pink florets that have violet shading at the tip. The hypanth has a diameter of less than 1cm and small, eyelash-like bracts. It forms large, beautiful hemispherical bushes, usually near the sea.

| 50-200cm ↑ → |

Chrysanthemum coronarium L.

Crown daisy

| 1 | 2 | 3 | 4 | 5 | 6 | 7 | 8 | 9 | 10 | 11 | 12 |

This large daisy can reach to 1 metre in height, with a strong, branched stem, and deeply-divided leaves. The flower-heads are up to 6cm in diameter with a yellow disc and ray florets that are white or yellow, or white in the upper half and yellow in the lower. Common on roadsides and in fields, and often cultivated as a decorative plant. The tender stems of this large daisy are edible, and it is also used to make a dye.

| 40-100cm ↑ |

Chrysanthemum segetum L.

Corn marigold

| 1 | 2 | 3 | 4 | 5 | 6 | 7 | 8 | 9 | 10 | 11 | 12 |

This resembles *C. coronarium*, but it always has yellow ray florets and toothed leaves, the lower ones with large lobes, the upper ones lanceolate. The brilliant yellow of the chrysanthemums has given the name to this genus, which is made up of two Greek words – *chrysós* meaning gold, and *ánthos* meaning flower.

| 20-60cm ↑ |

COMPOSITAE

`1` `2` `3` `4` `5` `6` `7` `8` `9` `10` `11` `12`

Cichorium intybus L.
Chicory

This is a very common plant with leaves arranged in rosettes, polymorphic and often deeply divided. The stem is tall, branched and slightly downy with heads growing from the axils formed by the branches. The florets are blue and toothed at the tips. An edible plant, much favoured by the Greeks who collect the young leaves that grow from the rosettes. The name is a very old one, since Theophrastus also called the plant *cichórion*.

| 30-120cm ↑ |

COMPOSITAE

`1` `2` `3` `4` `5` `6` `7` `8` `9` `10` `11` `12`

Cichorium spinosum L.
Spiny chicory

A spiny, much-branched phrygano plant with oblong leaves, toothed or with lobes. The leaves are eaten either fresh in a salad or boiled, and for this reason are keenly gathered. The heads resemble those of *C. intybus*, with a diameter of up to 3cm. The woody stems of the plant were used in bygone days to cover water jars in order to prevent insects from falling into them hence the popular name of the plant in Greek, *stamnangáthi* (*stámna* = water jar, *angáthi*= spine). Found in stony locations, from the sea right up to the mountain zone.

| 10-40cm ↑→ |

COMPOSITAE

`1` `2` `3` `4` `5` `6` `7` `8` `9` `10` `11` `12`

Cirsium creticum ssp. *creticum* (Lam) d' Urv.
Cirsium creticum ssp. creticum

This tall, branching plant has winged stems and wing-lobed leaves with very spiny lobes. The flower-bearing heads are ovate with a length of about 2cm and covered with scale-like bracts. The flowers are pink. Like the endemic *C. creticum* ssp. *dictaeum* which is found on the Lasithi High Plateau, this plant prefers damp locations.

| 0,50-1,50m ↑ |

Cirsium morinifolium BOISS. & HELDR.

COMPOSITAE

Cirsium morinifolium

1 2 3 4 5 6 7 8 9 10 11 12

This endemic thistle is distinguished among the plants of
the crevasses in the subalpine
zone by its height. It has a branching stem and smooth, deeply-divided
leaves with large spines. The flower-heads are
downy, spherical and up to 3cm in size. The
florets are pink or white (White Mountains).
The designation *morinifolium* refers to the
similarity of the leaves with those of *Morina
persica*. The plant is found in stony locations
in the great mountain massifs of Crete.

 | 0,60-1m ↑ | ▲▲ ⚘

Crepis auriculifolia SIEBER EX SPENGEL

COMPOSITAE

Crepis auriculifolia

1 2 3 4 5 6 7 8 9 10 11 12

A beautiful plant, relatively rare and endemic
to Crete. The leaves, which form impressive
rosettes, are leathery, smooth and bear the
characteristic teeth ('ears') which give it
its name. The flower-heads are up to 2cm
in diameter, with yellow florets. It is found
singly or in small groups in rocky locations
and on slopes, usually in the mountain zone.

| 20-30cm ↑ | ▲▲ ⚘ ◈

Crepis cretica BOISS. / syn. *C. neglecta* ssp. *cretica*

COMPOSITAE

Crepis cretica

1 2 3 4 5 6 7 8 9 10 11 12

A small, endemic plant with many thin stems
and leaves that are either deeply divided or
toothed, the lower ones stalked, the upper
ones stalkless. The flower-heads are up to
1cm in diameter with yellow florets and hairy
bracts. The small heads make recognition of
this plant easy since in all of the other species
they are considerably larger. Quite common
all over the island.

C. tybakiensis, also endemic, is more or less similar in
appearance with numerous leaves concentrated
at the base.

 | 10-30cm ↑ | ▲▲ ⚘ ◈

COMPOSITAE

| 1 | 2 | 3 | 4 | 5 | 6 | 7 | 8 | 9 | 10 | 11 | 12 |

Crepis rubra L.
Pink hawksbeard

More than 20 species of crepis are found in Greece, most of them with yellow flowers except for *C. rubra* which differs in that it alone has pink flowers. Its leaves are deeply divided or toothed, the upper ones are lanceolate. The heads with pink florets are up to 4cm in diameter. These 'wild dandelions' are edible and generally prefer stony locations.

| 10-40cm ↑ |

COMPOSITAE

| 1 | 2 | 3 | 4 | 5 | 6 | 7 | 8 | 9 | 10 | 11 | 12 |

Crepis sibthorpiana Boiss. & Heldr. ●
Crepis sibthorpiana

This little herbaceous plant is endemic to the large mountain massifs of western Crete and prefers stony locations in the mountain and alpine zone. The leaves are wing-lobed with fine down. The flower-heads are up to 2cm with yellow florets which have russet glints on the outside. The plant was named in honour of the botanist John Sibthorp (1758-1796) whose monumental work '*Flora Graeca*' is considered to be the rarest botanical publication in the world.

| 5-15cm ↑ |

COMPOSITAE

| 1 | 2 | 3 | 4 | 5 | 6 | 7 | 8 | 9 | 10 | 11 | 12 |

Crupina crupinastrum (Moris) Vis.
Crupina

An annual with a thin stem, sparsely branching, with solitary heads at the tips of the stems. The leaves are concentrated in the lower part of the plant, and are wing-like with toothed lobes. Pink florets, ovoid in the hypanth and with blackish-red bracts. Found in fields, phrygana, and stony locations.

| 20-60cm ↑ |

Dittrichia graveolens (L.) GREUTER / syn. *Inula graveolens*   COMPOSITAE
Stink aster

1	2	3	4	5	6	7	8	9	10	11	12

This is an annual plant, much-branched, and hairy, with stalkless narrow, sticky leaves. There are many flower-heads with a diameter of up to 1cm. The florets are yellow, surrounded by the bracts. The plant exudes a heavy odour of camphor, and was used in the past to repel insects. Found on roadsides, in ditches and abandoned fields.

| 20-50cm ↑ |

Dittrichia viscosa (L.) GREUTER/ syn. *Inula viscosa*   COMPOSITAE
Aromatic inula

1	2	3	4	5	6	7	8	9	10	11	12

This is the predominant wild flower in autumn. Often found on roadsides and in ditches, it is a decorative plant with its yellow, pyramid-shaped flower spikes. It has elongated leaves, which are lanceolate and sticky. The spike has many heads on long flower stalks. The florets are yellow, the ray florets tongue-like and toothed at the tip. A plant used as a dye, producing beautiful shades of green.

| 0,40-1m ↑ |

Echinops spinosissimus TURRA   COMPOSITAE
Spiny globe thistle

1	2	3	4	5	6	7	8	9	10	11	12

A perennial, with a smooth, white, branching stem. The leaves are deeply divided with spiny lobes. It has spherical flower-heads with white or bluish-violet florets surrounded by light green spiny bracts. Found in dry, stony locations. The name *Echinops* derives from the Greek and refers to the spiny appearance of the flower-heads.

| 0,50-1m ↑ |

COMPOSITAE

| 1 | 2 | 3 | 4 | 5 | 6 | 7 | 8 | 9 | 10 | 11 | 12 |

Erigeron glabratus HOPPE & HORNSCH.
Erigeron glabratus

A small, beau-ti-ful plant with smooth leaves, oblong-lanceolate, and eyelash-like. The stems are up to 10cm long with 1-2 flower-bearing heads, similar to those of the aster, which have a yellow disc and ribbon-like, light pink ray florets. The name *Erigeron* comes from the Greek words which mean 'old man's hair', and refers to the pappus of the plant, i.e. to the appearance of the head after the ripening of the seeds, which have hairs so that they can be dispersed by the wind.

| 10cm ↑ |

COMPOSITAE

| 1 | 2 | 3 | 4 | 5 | 6 | 7 | 8 | 9 | 10 | 11 | 12 |

Galactites tomentosa MOENCH.
Galactites

A common plant, taking its name from the white veins in the leaves which look as if they are filled with milk. It has an erect, downy stem and stalkless, deeply-divided leaves which are hairy on the underside and have spines at the tips of the lobes. The flower-head is ovoid with spiny bracts, covered with spidery hairs. The florets are pink or white. Found on roadsides, and in abandoned fields.

 | 30-80cm ↑ |

COMPOSITAE

| 1 | 2 | 3 | 4 | 5 | 6 | 7 | 8 | 9 | 10 | 11 | 12 |

Helichrysum doerfleri RECH. ●
Helichrysum

This little Helichrysum is a rare plant threatened with extinction, since its biotope extends over only a few square metres on Mount Thrypti in eastern Crete. It has short stems and oblong-lanceolate leaves, of which the upper ones are ovate, all covered with a dense white down. The flower-heads are very beautiful, with silvery-red bracts of a pearly texture. The florets are of a brilliant yellow colour, as is the case with all the Helichrysa, and it is this which gives the genus its name, deriving from the Greek words *helios* (sun) and *chrysós* (gold).

| 5-15cm → |

Helichrysum heldreichii Boiss.

Helichrysum heldreichii

| 1 | 2 | 3 | 4 | 5 | 6 | 7 | 8 | 9 | 10 | 11 | 12 |

A beautiful, much-branching shrub with elongated, linear leaves, silver-green in colour. The flowers are yellow and in dense flower-heads. The plant, which is endemic to western Crete, is found only in the Samaria and Aradena gorges and has been characterized as vulnerable. It prefers rocky slopes.

| 30-50cm →

Helichrysum italicum (Roth) G. Don fil. / syn. *H. microphyllum*

COMPOSITAE

Helichrysum italicum

| 1 | 2 | 3 | 4 | 5 | 6 | 7 | 8 | 9 | 10 | 11 | 12 |

This is one of the more widely distributed amaranths. It is a much-branched, aromatic plant, and has small, linear leaves covered with dense white down. The ovoid flower-bearing heads form dense clumps at the tips of the stems and have yellow florets, covered with greyish-yellow bracts. Found in stony places from the edge of the sea up to the mountain zone.

| 20-50cm ↑

Helichrysum stoechas (L.) Moench / syn. *H. barrelieri*

COMPOSITAE

Helichrysum stoechas

| 1 | 2 | 3 | 4 | 5 | 6 | 7 | 8 | 9 | 10 | 11 | 12 |

A perennial plant with many stems and narrow leaves. The whole plant is covered with dense white down. The flower-heads are cone-shaped and golden-yellow, surrounded by membrane-like bracts of the same colour in dense spikes. A very aromatic plant, particularly when the stem or leaves are cut. Found in phrygana and stony locations.

| 10-50cm ↑

1 | 2 | 3 | 4 | 5 | 6 | 7 | 8 | 9 | 10 | 11 | 12

Inula crithmoides L.
Golden samphire

This flowers in the autumn and prefers seashores and damp, brackish areas. It is a smooth plant with many erect stems and leaves in clusters, narrow and fleshy. The flower-heads measure from 2 to 3cm in size; the ray florets are yellow, the disc florets orange.

| 30-40cm ↑ |

COMPOSITAE

1 | 2 | 3 | 4 | 5 | 6 | 7 | 8 | 9 | 10 | 11 | 12

Lamyropsis cynaroides (Lam.) Dittrich
Lamyropsis cynaroides

A thistle with erect stems, covered with dense white down. The leaves are wing-lobed with spiny lobes, smooth on the upper surface and downy on the underside. The flower-heads are 3-4 cm in size with large thorny bracts and pink florets. Found in stony places.

| 30-50cm ↑ |

COMPOSITAE

1 | 2 | 3 | 4 | 5 | 6 | 7 | 8 | 9 | 10 | 11 | 12

Notobasis syriaca (L.) Cass.
Syrian thistle

A thistle with a robust stem similar to the 'gaidourángathi' (donkey thistle). The leaves are deeply divided, with white veins and spiny lobes, smooth on the upper surface, downy on the underside. Spherical heads with alternate bracts, needle-pointed, surrounded by large spines. The florets are all tubular and pink. Found in infertile, uncultivated locations.

| 20-120cm ↑ |

Onopordum bracteatum ssp. creticum Franco COMPOSITAE

Onopordum bracteatum ssp. creticum

1 2 3 4 5 6 7 8 9 10 11 12

A plant with a strong, grey-green, hairy and branching stem. The leaves are deeply divided with dense hair on the underside. The flower-heads are large – up to 7cm – and resemble those of the artichoke; they are covered with large, thorny bracts, a characteristic which gives the plant its name. There are numerous pink florets. The plant is endemic to Crete and found in dry, stony locations.

| 1-1,50m ↑ |

Onopordum illyricum L. COMPOSITAE

Illyrian Scotch thistle

1 2 3 4 5 6 7 8 9 10 11 12

The etymology of the names given to plants often shows an inclination towards humour; in the case of *Onopordum* (donkey thistle), for example, this is the scientific name assigned to it by *Linnaeus*. It comes from two Greek words, *ónos* = donkey and *pérdomai* = fart, which refer to the effect that it was supposed to have on the animal. *O. illyricum* has winged-lobed leaves which are spiny, and flower-heads up to 6cm with bracts shorter than the florets. Found in barren locations.

| 50-130cm ↑ |

Onopordum tauricum Willd. COMPOSITAE

Onopordum tauricum

1 2 3 4 5 6 7 8 9 10 11 12

This plant can reach a height of 2 metres. It has a spiny, winged stem. The leaves are large, deeply divided, hairy at first and then smooth. The heads are up to 7cm in size, spherical and with flat bracts at the base, longer than the pink florets. Found in abandoned fields, ditches and on roadsides.

| 1-2m ↑ |

COMPOSITAE

| 1 | 2 | 3 | 4 | 5 | 6 | 7 | 8 | 9 | 10 | 11 | 12 |

Otanthus maritimus (L.) HOFFMANNS. & LINK
Cottonweed

A perennial shrub with a preference for sandy coastlines, thus also for beaches. There are many erect stems, and lanceolate leaves, stalkless and entire. The whole plant is covered by dense, cotton-like down. The heads are round with tubular, yellow florets. The two swellings (little ears) at the base of the corolla give this plant its name, from the Greek words *otíon* (little ear) and *ánthos* (flower).

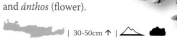

| 30-50cm ↑ |

COMPOSITAE

| 1 | 2 | 3 | 4 | 5 | 6 | 7 | 8 | 9 | 10 | 11 | 12 |

Pallenis spinosa (L.) CASS. / syn. *Asteriscus spinosus*
Pallenis spinosa

A biennial with branching stem, very downy. The leaves are elongated and lanceolate, downy, and concave, the upper ones stalkless. The flower-heads have spiny bracts, similar to the leaves, the inside bracts being shorter. The disc is yellow and up to 2cm, with ray florets that are tongue-shaped, yellow or russet-coloured. Found in fields, rocky locations, and olive groves.

| 20-60cm ↑ |

COMPOSITAE

| 1 | 2 | 3 | 4 | 5 | 6 | 7 | 8 | 9 | 10 | 11 | 12 |

Phagnalon graecum BOIS. & HELDR.
Phagnalon

A perennial phrygano plant with many stems and oblong-lanceolate leaves with undulating edges, all very downy. The flower-heads are at the tips of the stems, solitary, and are rounded with narrow, needle-like bracts which are pointed at the tips, and yellow florets. It is usually found on rocky slopes.

| 10-40cm ↑ |

Phagnalon pygmaeum (Sieber) Greuter / syn. *P. pumilum*   COMPOSITAE
Phagnalon pygmaeum

1 2 3 4 5 6 7 8 9 10 11 12

This small, endemic plant is found in the mountain and alpine zone, particularly in the White Mountains. The heads are solitary, on thin flower-stalks, with light yellow florets. The leaves are spatulate, smooth or covered with dense white down. Found in stony places and in clefts in the rocks.

 | 10-15cm ↑ | ◮ ⚓ ◈

Picnomon acarna (L.) Cass.   COMPOSITAE
Picnomon

1 2 3 4 5 6 7 8 9 10 11 12

An annual plant, very spiny and with a winged, branching stem. The leaves are lanceolate with many spines on the lips. The flower-heads are hidden by bracts similar in appearance to the leaves. The florets are pink. Found in stony places and infertile fields. The plants, when they have shrivelled, take on a golden colour and decorate the roadsides for a long time.

 | 50-70cm ↑ | ◮ ⚓

Ptilostemon chamaepeuce (L.) Less.   COMPOSITAE
Shrubby ptilostemon

1 2 3 4 5 6 7 8 9 10 11 12

This small, downy shrub has very characteristic needle-like leaves, similar to those of the pine. The heads are ovoid with scale-like downy bracts, sharply pointed. The florets are tubular, pink and more rarely white. Found on steep rocky cliffs and slopes. The name of this elegant plant epitomizes the use of Greek words in the nomenclature of plants.

| 30-100cm ↑ | ◮ ◭ ◼

Scolymus hispanicus L.
Spanish oyster plant

An annual herbaceous plant with branching, winged stems, very spiny. The leaves are wing-lobed, spiny and with white veining. The flower-heads grow from the axils of the stems and have spiny bracts and tongue-like yellow florets. Both the tender stems of the plant and the roots are edible. Found in barren places, from the sea up to the semi-mountainous zone.

| 20-80cm ↑ |

Scorzonera cretica L. ●
Cretan viper's grass

A variform, perennial herbaceous plant with many stems, erect and downy. The narrow, linear leaves are up to 1cm in width, most of them concentrated at the base of the plant. The heads are brownish-red with all the florets yellow and tongue-like. Found on slopes, roadsides, and in rocky places.

| 20-30cm ↑ |

Senecio fruticulosus Sm. ●
Senecio fruticulosus

The appearance of this plant does not justify its name ('*fruticulosus*' = 'shrubby'), since it is a small, perennial herbaceous plant with inverse-ovate leaves that are smooth and toothed. The flower-heads have a diameter of up to 2cm with a yellow disc and peripheral florets. It is endemic to Crete and found in the mountain and alpine zone, usually in the shade of other shrubs.

| 10-30cm → |

Senecio rupestris WALDST. & KIT.

Senecio rupestris

COMPOSITAE

1 2 3 4 5 6 7 8 9 10 11 12

A perennial, much-branching plant with wing-lobed leaves. The flower-heads are up to 2cm in size, with tongue-like florets and a yellow disc. It is relatively rare and found in stony locations and on rocky slopes up to the mountain zone.

| 10-40cm ↑ |

Silybum marianum (L.) GAERTN.

Holy thistle, milk thistle

COMPOSITAE

1 2 3 4 5 6 7 8 9 10 11 12

A biennial plant, with strongly-branched, wand-like stems. The leaves are large with undulating, spiny edges and develop in rosettes during the first year. According to tradition, the white spots and veins of the plant were caused by the milk of the Virgin Mary – hence the name *marianum*. The heads have large, spiny bracts and all of the florets are tubular and pink in colour. Found on the margins of fields, in ditches, and on roadsides.

| 20-150cm ↑ |

● *Staehelina arborea* SCHREB. / syn. *Staehelina petiolata*

Staehelina arborea

COMPOSITAE

1 2 3 4 5 6 7 8 9 10 11 12

A small bush with a woody stem which gives it a tree-like form. The leaves are typically long, downy-stalked, large, ovate, smooth and green on the upper surface, with white down on the underside. The heads are oblong, cylindrical and scaly with all florets cylindrical, and pink in colour. This plant is usually found in ravines, where it prefers sheer slopes and crevices in the rocks.

| 20-80cm ↑ |

COMPOSITAE

1 2 3 4 5 6 7 8 9 10 11 12

Staehelina fruticosa L. ●

Staehelina fruticosa

A small bush or phrygano plant with lanceolate leaves which are smooth, fleshy and many in number, the lower ones having a little stalk. The flower-bearing heads resemble those of *S. arborea*, but the florets are white and it flowers later. Found in similar biotopes.

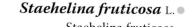

| 20-100cm ↑ |

COMPOSITAE

1 2 3 4 5 6 7 8 9 10 11 12

Tragopogon hybridus L. / syn. *Geropogon hybridus*

Tragopogon hybridus

A plant with a thin, smooth stem, and periblastic leaves which are straight-lanceolate, pointed at the tip. The heads have 5-8 bracts, at least double the number of the light pink florets which themselves occur in an even number. The whole appearance of the flower resembles that of a star. Found in fields, meadows, and on roadsides.

| 20-50cm ↑ |

COMPOSITAE

1 2 3 4 5 6 7 8 9 10 11 12

Tragopogon porrifolius L. / syn. *Tragopogon sinuatus*

Salsify, Goat's Beard

A more robust plant than the latter with broad, linear, periblastic leaves. The flower-heads contain many florets, pink or violet with sharply-pointed bracts which are either the same length or longer than the ray florets. After flowering, the bracts close and re-open to release the winged seeds. The roots of the plant are edible. It is common in the lowland zone.

| 20-80cm ↑ |

Calystegia sepium (L.) R. Br.
Hedge bindweed

1	2	3	4	5	6	7	8	9	10	11	12

A perennial climber with large dart- to heart-shaped and slightly undulating leaves. The flowers are white, solitary and up to 5cm with a short stalk, growing in the leaf axils. A very decorative plant which is often cultivated on fences. Found in moist, shady areas, by streams, and in thickets. The two bracts which enclose the calyx like a roof give the name to this plant (calyx + *stégi*, i.e. roof).

| 1-3m ↑ →

Convolvulus althaeoides L.
Mallow-leaved bindweed

1	2	3	4	5	6	7	8	9	10	11	12

A perennial plant, hairy, normally trailing or a climber. The leaves take a number of forms; the lower ones are heart-shaped with shallow lobes, the upper ones palm-lobed with a larger central lobe. The flowers resemble those of *Calystegia* – pink and darker at the centre. The two bracts are of a rather lower height than that of the calyx. Found in rocky locations and on slopes.

| 50-100cm ↑ →

● *Convolvulus argyrothamnos* Greuter
Convolvulus argyrothamnos

1	2	3	4	5	6	7	8	9	10	11	12

This extremely rare plant is endemic to Crete and numbers only a few individuals. The leaves are elongated and silver in colour – hence the name. The flowers are in dense terminal inflorescences with a white, bell-shaped corolla up to 4cm in diameter which is retained during the flowering period. The plant, which has been characterized as endangered, is found on the vertical slopes of the gorges.

| 40-80cm ↑

| 1 | 2 | 3 | 4 | 5 | 6 | 7 | 8 | 9 | 10 | 11 | 12 |

Convolvulus arvensis L.
Field bindweed

A creeping or climbing plant with thin stems and dart-like leaves. The flowers are white, pink or two-coloured with a long flower-stalk, in the leaf axils. The calyx has rounded lobes. Common in fields, along fences, and in olive groves.

| 0,5-2m ↑ → |

| 1 | 2 | 3 | 4 | 5 | 6 | 7 | 8 | 9 | 10 | 11 | 12 |

Convolvulus dorycnium L. ●
Convolvulus dorycnium

A perennial, much-branching, downy shrub which forms impressive hemispherical masses. The leaves are small and lanceolate. The flowers are numerous, white or pink on a long flower-stalk. Found in infertile and dry locations, usually near the sea and more rarely in the hinterland.

| 50-100cm ↑ |

| 1 | 2 | 3 | 4 | 5 | 6 | 7 | 8 | 9 | 10 | 11 | 12 |

Convolvulus elegantissimus MILL.
Convolvulus elegantissimus

This plant resembles C. althaeoides and is considered a subspecies of the latter by some authorities. It differs in the colour of the leaves which are silvery-green, and in the flowers which are light-coloured at the centre. Found on roadsides, slopes and cliffs.

| 50-100cm ↑ → |

Convolvulus oleifolius DESR.
Convolvulus oleifolius

1	2	3	4	5	6	7	8	9	10	11	12

A perennial with a woody stem and leaves which are lanceolate-straight, silver in colour and resembling those of the olive. The flowers are light pink and up to 3cm in diameter, in terminal spikes. Found in stony locations and phrygana, often near the sea.

| 10-50cm ↑→ |

Convolvulus siculus L.
Small blue convolvulus

1	2	3	4	5	6	7	8	9	10	11	12

An annual, herbaceous plant with large, heart-shaped leaves, stalked and slightly hairy. The flowers are small, up to to 1.5cm, axillary, solitary and on a long flower-stalk. The bracts are longer than the lobes of the calyx. The corolla is blue with a light yellow throat. Found in stony places and gorges.

| 20-50cm ↑ |

Cuscuta atrans FEINBRUN
Cuscuta atrans

1	2	3	4	5	6	7	8	9	10	11	12

The cuscutas are parasitic plants with thin, thread-like stems which wind around the stems of other plants, often presenting a comet-like appearance. Five species grow on Crete, of which only *C. atrans* is endemic. It has bright red stems and small white flowers in spherical inflorescences. It is found in the subalpine and alpine zone on spiny shrubs, such as *Berberis cretica* in the photograph.

| 20-50cm ↑ |

CRASSULACEAE

| 1 | 2 | 3 | 4 | 5 | 6 | 7 | 8 | 9 | 10 | 11 | 12 |

Rosularia serrata (L.) A. BERGER
Rosularia serrata

A fleshy plant resembling *Umbilicus*. It has an erect stem with ovate, fleshy leaves that are stalkless and arranged in a basal rosette. The flowers have stalks; they are five-part, bell-like, and white with red stippling. The lobes and calyx are sharply-pointed. There are loose flower–spikes along the whole length of the stem. Normally found in shady places, on rocky slopes.

| 1030cm ↑ |

CRASSULACEAE

| 1 | 2 | 3 | 4 | 5 | 6 | 7 | 8 | 9 | 10 | 11 | 12 |

Sedum album L.
White stonecrop

The Sedum family comprises herbaceous plants with fleshy leaves known by the common folk name of 'amaranths'. *S. album* has an erect stem with alternate, ovate leaves, flat on the upper surface. The flowers have five white or slightly pinkish petals with pink veining, and develop in terminal clusters. The plant often grows in dense clumps. Found in rocky locations in the mountain and alpine zone.

| 10-30cm ↑ |

CRASSULACEAE

| 1 | 2 | 3 | 4 | 5 | 6 | 7 | 8 | 9 | 10 | 11 | 12 |

Sedum amplexicaule DC.
Sedum amplexicaule

The subspecies *tenuifolium* is found on Crete. It is a perennial plant with slender stems, which may or may not be flower-bearing, and small round leaves, of which those on the fertile stems are periblastic. The flowers are up to 1.5cm in size, in heads at the tips of the stems. There are 5-10 yellow petals. Found on rocky slopes and in phrygana.

| 10-20cm ↑ |

Sedum creticum C. Presl
Sedum creticum

CRASSULACEAE

| 1 | 2 | 3 | 4 | 5 | 6 | 7 | 8 | 9 | 10 | 11 | 12 |

A biennial plant with a russet-coloured, erect stem and spatulate, fleshy leaves concentrated in a basal rosette. The flowers are whitish-pink with sharply pointed petals in a pyramidal inflorescence. The rosette develops in the first year and the stem bearing the flower in the second. Found on rocky slopes.

 | 8-15cm ↑ |

Sedum laconicum Greuter
Sedum laconicum

CRASSULACEAE

| 1 | 2 | 3 | 4 | 5 | 6 | 7 | 8 | 9 | 10 | 11 | 12 |

A dwarf plant with leaves of up to 1cm, ovate and fleshy. The flowers are axillary, yellow and have lanceolate petals twice as long as the sepals. Found in rocky places and rock-crevices. The subspecies *praesidis* is endemic to Crete and also classified as a separate species under the name *Sedum praesidis*.

 | 5-10cm ↑ |

Sedum littoreum Guss.
Sedum littoreum

CRASSULACEAE

| 1 | 2 | 3 | 4 | 5 | 6 | 7 | 8 | 9 | 10 | 11 | 12 |

A small fleshy plant with a stem that is thinner at the base and spoon-shaped leaves with russet stippling. The flowers are yellow with linear, lanceolate petals, sharply pointed at the tip, and sepals which are a little shorter. Found normally on rocks and, despite its name, it is met right up to the mountain zone.

 | 5-10cm ↑ |

CRASSULACEAE

| 1 | 2 | 3 | 4 | 5 | 6 | 7 | 8 | 9 | 10 | 11 | 12 |

Sedum rubens L.
Sedum rubens

A plant with a low habit, glandular and hairy with russet-coloured fleshy leaves, the lower ones opposite, often in rosettes, and the upper ones alternate. The flowers resemble those of *S. album* but the petals are sharply pointed at the tip. Found at all altitudes, normally in rock crevices.

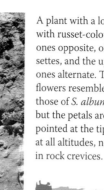

| 5-15cm ↑ |

CRASSULACEAE

| 1 | 2 | 3 | 4 | 5 | 6 | 7 | 8 | 9 | 10 | 11 | 12 |

Umbilicus horizontalis (Guss.) DC.
Pennywort

A perennial, russet-coloured fleshy plant with a flower-spike in a long cluster and small tubular flowers, horizontally carried and with a short calyx. The leaves at the base are stalked, kidney-shaped, and sparsely toothed, the upper ones small and straight like bracts. Found in rocky locations, in walls and amidst ruins.

U. rupestris is similar but has drooping flowers and a calyx extending up to the middle of the corolla.

| 10-50cm ↑ |

CRASSULACEAE

| 1 | 2 | 3 | 4 | 5 | 6 | 7 | 8 | 9 | 10 | 11 | 12 |

Umbilicus parviflorus (Desf.) DC.
Small-flowered navelwort

A perennial, fleshy plant with an erect stem, russet-coloured and with fleshy, kidney-shaped leaves, the lower ones stalked, the upper ones almost periblastic. The flowers are small and grow in short axillary clusters. The petals are yellow and double the length of the sepals. Found in rocky locations, and in dry stone walls. The name derives from the Latin word *umbilicus* ('navel'), and refers to the shape of the leaves.

| 10-40cm ↑ |

Aethionema saxatile ssp. *creticum* (L.) R. Br

Burnt candytuft

A perennial plant, much-branched and with a woody base. The leaves are ovate or lanceolate and fleshy, growing along the whole length of the stem, with the flowers in dense clusters at the tip. There are 4 petals, pink or white. Normally found on rocky slopes in the mountain zone. The unusual name of the plant derives from the leaves which at maturity appear burnt; it comes from the Greek *aithó* (to burn) and *níma* (thread), the latter referring to its thin stems.

CRUCIFERAE

| 10-25cm ↑ → |

● *Alyssum fragillimum* (Bald.) Rech.

Alyssum fragillimum

CRUCIFERAE

A dwarf, creeping, perennial plant endemic to the White Mountains. The leaves are ovate-lanceolate, fleshy and hairy, up to 1.5cm in length. The tiny, yellow flowers grow in a dense inflorescence. The plant, which prefers stony locations in the alpine zone, has been characterized as vulnerable.

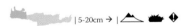

| 5-20cm → |

Alyssum saxatile L. / syn. *Aurinia saxatilis*

Golden alyssum

CRUCIFERAE

The most frequently occurring of its family, *A. saxatile* is a perennial plant, polymorphic, with stalked lower leaves which are lanceolate with shallow lobes, and upper leaves that are lanceolate and stalkless. The flowers are arranged in terminal clusters and have 4 brilliant yellow petals, which are two-lobed. As its name suggests, the plant prefers rocky locations and is found frequently on slopes in the mountain zone.

| 10-30cm ↑ |

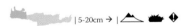

CRUCIFERAE

Alyssum simplex RUDOLFI / syn. *Alyssum minus*
Alyssum simplex

| 1 | 2 | 3 | 4 | 5 | 6 | 7 | 8 | 9 | 10 | 11 | 12 |

A small, annual plant with stalkless leaves which are lanceolate, downy, fleshy and sharply pointed. Small yellow flowers in a dense hemispherical inflorescence. The plant, which is more often found in eastern Crete, prefers stony locations and gorges.

| 5-20cm ↑ |

CRUCIFERAE

Alyssum sphacioticum BOISS. & HELDR. ●
Alyssum sphacioticum

| 1 | 2 | 3 | 4 | 5 | 6 | 7 | 8 | 9 | 10 | 11 | 12 |

This is a small, much-branching plant with stems which do not exceed 10cm in length. It is found only on some peaks of the White Mountains, above 2100m. The leaves are up to 1cm in length, ovate-spatulate and hairy, along almost the whole length of the stem. The flowers are small and yellow in a loose raceme. It is found in stony places in the alpine zone and has been characterized as vulnerable. The other two great mountain massifs of Crete have their own endemic plants – *A. idaeum* (Idi), and *A. lassithicum* (Dikti).

| 5-15cm ↑ |

CRUCIFERAE

Arabis alpina L.
Arabis alpina

| 1 | 2 | 3 | 4 | 5 | 6 | 7 | 8 | 9 | 10 | 11 | 12 |

This little herbaceous plant is a perennial which prefers alpine altitudes. It is densely haired with ovate-spatulate leaves that are lightly toothed and arranged in small rosettes. The stems are erect with flowers in loose clusters. The flowers have 4 petals, up to 1cm, and are white; their length is double that of the sepals. The plant is normally found in rock crevices.

| 10-35cm ↑ |

Aubrieta deltoidea D.C.
Aubrieta

| 1 | 2 | 3 | 4 | 5 | 6 | 7 | 8 | 9 | 10 | 11 | 12 |

This is one of the most beautiful wild flowers of the mountain zone. It is a grassy plant and often forms little cushions. The leaves are spatulate-rhomboidal, downy and loosely toothed. The flowers are violet or pink with a yellow throat. Two of the 4 sepals bear a little swelling. It is to be found in rock crevices, and is often cultivated as a decorative plant.

| 10-20cm ↑→ |

Biscutella didyma L.
Biscutella didyma

| 1 | 2 | 3 | 4 | 5 | 6 | 7 | 8 | 9 | 10 | 11 | 12 |

This little herbaceous plant is distinguished by its very typical twinned, disc-shaped husks of which each contains one seed. It is an annual, erect and hairy with polymorphic leaves concentrated at the base. The flowers are arranged in clusters and have yellow petals. Found in rocky places, fallow fields, and phrygana.

| 10-40cm ↑ |

Brassica cretica LAM.
Brassica cretica

| 1 | 2 | 3 | 4 | 5 | 6 | 7 | 8 | 9 | 10 | 11 | 12 |

A herbaceous plant with large, fleshy grey-green leaves. The flowers have 4 white or whitish-yellow petals in a large, dense and erect cluster. This is an impressive plant which prefers sheer, rocky slopes. It is edible and particularly during difficult times in the past has constituted a basic dietary component along with other wild greens.

| 40-60cm ↑ |

CRUCIFERAE

1 2 3 4 5 6 7 8 9 10 11 12

Brassica nigra (L.) W.D.J. Koch
Brassica nigra

A plant resembling
B. cretica, but with
even larger leaves. The
flowers are yellow and
arranged in an erect,
dense raceme. It is
edible and thus often
cultivated, also for its seeds
which were once used in the
preparation of mustard. Found
in rocky places.

| 40-80cm ↑ |

CRUCIFERAE

1 2 3 4 5 6 7 8 9 10 11 12

Cakile maritima Scop.
Sea rocket

This is an annual, smooth
plant, with branching
stems which are either trailing
or climbing, and fleshy leaves,
deeply divided and with
lobes of uneven length that
often have yellowish-red shading.
The flower has 4 petals that are
white or have slight violet shading
and an equal number of unlobed
sepals, two of them with a hump.
In folk medicine the plant is used as a
diuretic. It is common on sandy beaches.

| 20-50cm ↑ → |

CRUCIFERAE

1 2 3 4 5 6 7 8 9 10 11 12

Cardaria draba (L.) Desv. / syn. *Lepidium draba*
Hoary cress

A tall plant with strong, branching stems,
common on roadsides and amongst rubble. The leaves are wide, ovate or lanceolate,
and toothed; the lower ones are stalked, the upper
ones periblastic. The flowers are
small and numerous, white
and in a fan-shaped head.
The name of the genus
derives from the Greek word
kardiá ('heart') and refers to the
shape of the pericarp, while *draba*
originates from Dioscurides.

| 50-100cm ↑ |

Erysimum candicum ssp. candicum SNOGERUP CRUCIFERAE
Erysimum candicum

| 1 | 2 | 3 | 4 | 5 | 6 | 7 | 8 | 9 | 10 | 11 | 12 |

This plant with its robust stem prefers steep rocky slopes and flowers from February onwards. The leaves are narrow, lanceolate and have a strong, light-coloured vein; they are up to 15cm in length. Most of them are concentrated at the base and form a rosette. The flowers are in terminal clusters and have 4 brilliant yellow petals and green sepals.

| 20-40cm ↑ |

Erysimum creticum BOISS. & HELDR. CRUCIFERAE
Erysimum creticum

| 1 | 2 | 3 | 4 | 5 | 6 | 7 | 8 | 9 | 10 | 11 | 12 |

A biennial plant with an erect, branching stem. The upper leaves are almost linear, the lower ones much larger, toothed and concave. Flowers yellow, in dense, terminal racemes. The plant is endemic to eastern Crete, and found in stony places and on slopes. One such biotope where it can be found is that of the Kapsa Monastery ravine.

| 30-50cm ↑ |

Erysimum mutabile BOISS. & HELDR. CRUCIFERAE
Erysimum mutabile

| 1 | 2 | 3 | 4 | 5 | 6 | 7 | 8 | 9 | 10 | 11 | 12 |

A perennial, with thin, erect or creeping stems. The leaves are lanceolate-spatulate, the lower ones arranged in a rosette. The flowers have yellow petals which are brown on the outside. The plant is found in the mountain and subalpine zone in rocky places and low thickets.

| 10-20cm → ↑ |

CRUCIFERAE

| 1 | 2 | 3 | 4 | 5 | 6 | 7 | 8 | 9 | 10 | 11 | 12 |

Erysimum raulinii Boiss. ●

Erysimum raulinii

A biennial plant with an erect quadrangular stem and large lanceolate leaves similar to those of *E. candicum*, the lower leaves in a rosette. The flowers are yellow, fragrant, and arranged in a dense terminal raceme. Endemic to western Crete and found in cypress forests, on rocky slopes, and in phrygana.

 | 20-40cm ↑ | 🔺 ⚓

CRUCIFERAE

| 1 | 2 | 3 | 4 | 5 | 6 | 7 | 8 | 9 | 10 | 11 | 12 |

Malcolmia flexuosa Sibth. & Sm. ●

Malcolmia flexuosa

An annual, slightly downy with fleshy, ovate-elliptical leaves. The flowers have a diameter of up to 2.5cm, with 4 pink or violet petals which have dark veining and a yellow throat. The seeds are in flexible pods with a length of up to 8cm. Normally found on sands and rocks near the sea.

 | 10-35cm ↑ | 🔺 ⚓

CRUCIFERAE

| 1 | 2 | 3 | 4 | 5 | 6 | 7 | 8 | 9 | 10 | 11 | 12 |

Matthiola sinuata (L.) R.Br.

Sea stock

A biennial plant, erect and with many leaves at the base which are deeply divided, with round lobes and a lip that is turned upwards, whence it derives its name. The upper leaves are linear and undulating. The flowers are violet and pleasantly-scented, up to 2.5cm in diameter. A beautiful plant, which prefers rocky slopes near the sea. It is cultivated for decoration.

 | 20-80cm ↑ | 🔺 ⚓ ◆ 🌿

Matthiola tricuspidata (L.) R.Br.
Three-horned stock

1 2 3 4 5 6 7 8 9 10 11 12

An annual with herbaceous-type stems, erect or trailing. The leaves are downy, deeply divided with round lobes. The flower has a diameter of up to 1.5cm and is pink or violet, lighter-coloured at the centre. The husk which encloses the fruit has three horns at the apex, a characteristic which gives its name to the plant. Found near the sea, on sand or on rocky promontories.

| 7-40cm ↑ |

Sinapis alba L.
White mustard

1 2 3 4 5 6 7 8 9 10 11 12

An annual with numerous, branching stems and large billowy leaves with toothed lobes. The flowers are yellow. The plant is found in fields, olive groves and on roadsides, often in large populations. The Cretans gather the tender shoots of the plant ('*vrouvoxéstaha*').

| 30-100cm ↑ |

Bryonia cretica L.
White bryony

1 2 3 4 5 6 7 8 9 10 11 12

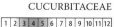

A unisexual plant, hairy and climbing with the help of spiral tendrils similar to those of the vine. It has palmately-lobed leaves with white veining, lighter-coloured on the underside. The flowers are yellow-green with dark veining and the seed pod is red. In the female plants the inflorescences do not contain more than 1 or 2 flowers. This is a poisonous plant which prefers hedges and thickets.

| 1-4m ↑ |

CUCURBITACEAE

| 1 | 2 | 3 | 4 | 5 | 6 | 7 | 8 | 9 | 10 | 11 | 12 |

Ecballium elaterium Rich.

Squirting cucumber

A trailing perennial herbaceous plant, fleshy and very bristly with triangular leaves, toothed and hairy on the underside. The flowers are yellow and bloom in the leaf axils, the male flowers in clusters, the female flowers singly. Of particular interest is the way in which the plant disperses its seeds. The fruit is very sensitive and at the slightest touch it bursts like a little bomb and throws its seeds far away; it 'uncoils' like a watch-spring. This is a poisonous plant with uses in folk medicine. It is common in fallow fields, amidst rubble, and on roadsides.

 | 30-100cm → |

DIPSACACEAE

| 1 | 2 | 3 | 4 | 5 | 6 | 7 | 8 | 9 | 10 | 11 | 12 |

Pterocephalus papposus (L.) Coult.

Pterocephalus papposus

This is an annual, downy and with an erect stem and deeply-divided leaves with toothed or entire lobes, the central one being larger. The flower-heads have large pointed bracts and pink flowers with five lobes. Found in phrygana and thickets.

| 10-50cm ↑ |

DIPSACACEAE   # *Scabiosa maritima* L. / syn. *S. atropurpurea, Sixalix atropurpurea*

| 1 | 2 | 3 | 4 | 5 | 6 | 7 | 8 | 9 | 10 | 11 | 12 |

Mournful widow

Despite the name, this plant is found at greater altitudes. It has long, slender stems and dissected leaves; the upper leaves are entire. The flower-heads are up to 5cm in diameter; the florets have five lobes and are violet, pink or white in colour, the ray florets being much larger. Found in dry, wasteland locations.

Knautia integrifolia. Plants of this genus resemble the scabiouses, but they are easily differentiated by their florets, which have four lobes.

 | 20-60cm ↑ |

Scabiosa sphaciotica Loem. & Schult. / syn. *Lomelosia sphaciotica*   DIPSACACEAE

Scabiosa sphaciotica

| 1 | 2 | 3 | 4 | 5 | 6 | 7 | 8 | 9 | 10 | 11 | 12 |

A creeping plant with a plethora of shoots and very characteristic dense, deeply-divided leaves with small lobes, ovate and very hairy. The flower-heads are up to 1.5cm in size, white or slightly violet-tinged with no more than 8 peripheral florets. Endemic to Crete, and found in stony places in the alpine zone.

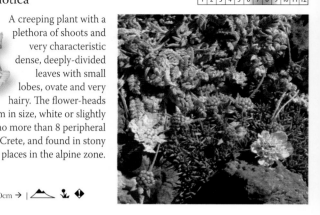

| 10-40cm →

Tremastelma palaestinum (L.) Janch. / syn. *Lomelosia brachiata*   DIPSACACEAE

Tremastelma

| 1 | 2 | 3 | 4 | 5 | 6 | 7 | 8 | 9 | 10 | 11 | 12 |

A small, annual, hairy herbaceous plant with an erect, downy stem. The leaves are hairy and lanceolate. The flower-heads have a diameter of up to 2 cm with pink florets, the outer lobes extremely large. The calyx, which has 10 tough, hairy lobes, is very characteristic. Found in stony places.

| 10-40cm ↑

Arbutus andrachne L.

ERICACEAE

Eastern strawberry tree

| 1 | 2 | 3 | 4 | 5 | 6 | 7 | 8 | 9 | 10 | 11 | 12 |

This plant has dark green leaves which are lanceolate, slightly toothed, and membranous. The flowers are small and off-white, in short inflorescences. The fruits are smaller than those of *A. unedo* and are not edible. Of particular interest is the trunk which sheds its thin skin in long strips to reveal an impressive red and silky-textured surface.

| 2- 5m ↑

ERICACEAE

| 1 | 2 | 3 | 4 | 5 | 6 | 7 | 8 | 9 | 10 | 11 | 12 |

Arbutus unedo L.
Strawberry tree

A beautiful bush or tree with light green leaves, lanceolate and slightly toothed. The flowers are white or pink, bell-shaped and arranged in dense nodding spikes which appear in autumn or sometimes in spring; thus the simultaneous occurrence of fruits and flowers is not rare. The fruits – the arbutus berries – are red, spherical with a diameter of up to 2cms and very tasty. The tree is found in thickets in Mediterranean maquis, often in large populations.

| 1,5-10m ↑ |

ERICACEAE

| 1 | 2 | 3 | 4 | 5 | 6 | 7 | 8 | 9 | 10 | 11 | 12 |

Erica arborea L.
Tree heath

A much-branching shrub and more rarely tree with small, linear leaves, growing in whorls. The flowers are small, white, bell-shaped and fragrant, with a relatively long flower stalk in a pyramid-like fan. This is one of the species which characterises the so-called Mediterranean maquis.

| 1-4m ↑ |

ERICACEAE

| 1 | 2 | 3 | 4 | 5 | 6 | 7 | 8 | 9 | 10 | 11 | 12 |

Erica manipuliflora SALISB.
Erica manipuliflora

Autumn heather is a small phryga-no-like shrub, either spreading or erect in habit, much-branched with a woody base. The leaves are small and linear, grass-green in colour and arranged in whorls. The flowers are numerous and small, bell-like and pink in long spikes. Found in thickets and phrygana, often covering large areas and giving colour to a monotonous autumnal landscape.

| 20-80cm ↑ |

Euphorbia acanthothamnos Heldr. & Sart. ex Boiss.   EUPHORBIACEAE
Greek spiny spurge

| 1 | 2 | 3 | 4 | 5 | 6 | 7 | 8 | 9 | 10 | 11 | 12 |

A perennial, cushion-like shrub with many spiny branches. The leaves are elliptical and up to 2cm long, with the bracts like a cup. The umbel has 3-4 rays which in the year after flowering transform into spines. It is common in stony locations and probably endemic to Greece. The name comes from the Greek meaning 'thorny bush' and gives an accurate picture of this plant.

| 10-30cm ↑ | ▲ ☁ ☠

Euphorbia characias L.   EUPHORBIACEAE
Large Mediterranean spurge

| 1 | 2 | 3 | 4 | 5 | 6 | 7 | 8 | 9 | 10 | 11 | 12 |

The most common of the euphorbiae, this is a plant with many erect, strong stems, which are denuded at the base. The leaves are numerous, grey, lanceolate and elongated. The umbel is dense and the cups hemispherical with dark red glands. The name originates from Dioscurides and refers to the stony or rocky biotopes preferred by the plant (*hárakas* = rock).

| 30-80cm ↑ | ▲ ⚘ ☠

Euphorbia dendroides L.   EUPHORBIACEAE
Tree spurge

| 1 | 2 | 3 | 4 | 5 | 6 | 7 | 8 | 9 | 10 | 11 | 12 |

One of the more beautiful euphorbiae with thick, denuded stems which give a tree-like appearance to the plant. The leaves are lanceolate and elongated; after flowering they take on an orange shade and thereafter, during the course of the summer, are shed. The umbel has a few rays and yellowish-green bracts, triangular and interdivided. Found in rocky and infertile areas, often in large populations.

| 0,5-2m ↑ | ▲ ♣ ☠

EUPHORBIACEAE

| 1 | 2 | 3 | 4 | 5 | 6 | 7 | 8 | 9 | 10 | 11 | 12 |

Euphorbia helioscopia L.
Sun spurge

This is an annual with a smooth, erect stem, and yellow-green leaves, ovate and finely toothed; the upper leaves are larger. The umbels have 5 rays and bracts similar to the leaves. The name comes from Dioscurides and refers to the ability of the plant to turn towards the sun.

| 10-50cm ↑ |

EUPHORBIACEAE

| 1 | 2 | 3 | 4 | 5 | 6 | 7 | 8 | 9 | 10 | 11 | 12 |

Euphorbia herniariifolia WILLD.
Euphorbia herniariifolia

This dwarf euphorbia has ovate, sharply-pointed grey leaves which cover the creeping stems. The umbel has 4-5 rays and bracts similar to the leaves. The fruits have fluked segments, a characteristic which distinguishes it from the similar-looking *E. rechingeri*, the fruits of which have spherical segments. Found in stony places at high altitudes.

| 5-15cm → |

EUPHORBIACEAE

| 1 | 2 | 3 | 4 | 5 | 6 | 7 | 8 | 9 | 10 | 11 | 12 |

Euphorbia paralias L.
Sea spurge

The beautiful Greek name of this plant was given to it by Theophrastus, and accurately describes its preferred biotope of sandy beaches. It is a perennial, with a stout stem, branching from the root, often a strong russet colour. The leaves are numerous, along almost the whole length of the stems; they are grey, straight-lanceolate, the upper ones broader. The umbel is round with 6 rays at the most, and the umbels have concave, ovate bracts.

| 20-60cm ↑ |

Euphorbia peplis L.
Purple spurge

This little euphorbia shares the same biotopes as *E. paralias* since it is found, sometimes completely buried, on sandy beaches. It is a creeping plant with robust russet-coloured stems and opposite, ovate, fleshy leaves, almost stalkless and reddish-green in colour. The name '*peplis*' originates from Dioscurides.

| 10-20cm →

• *Euphorbia rechingeri* GREUTER
Euphorbia rechingeri

EUPHORBIACEAE

This is a dwarf plant, endemic to the White Mountains. It has greyish-blue, ovate, pointed leaves. The flowers are russet-coloured with five rays and bracts similar to the leaves. The fruits are unlobed. It is found above 1800 metres in stony locations and in rock-clefts. It is such a small plant that it sometimes goes unnoticed.

| 5-10cm →

Ricinus communis L.
Castor oil plant

EUPHORBIACEAE

A perennial plant with an erect stem and palm-lobed leaves, often russet-coloured with toothed lanceolate lobes. The clusters of hairy, red balls are in reality curious flower-spikes of female flowers without petals. Dioscurides named it *króton* (the ancient Greek word for 'tick') because the seed resembles an animal tick. The seeds are rich in oil (ricinus) which is used for manufacturing and pharmaceutical purposes. *R. communis* is often cultivated in gardens as a decorative plant and it is believed to repel insects. It is self-sowing, often on roadsides and in ravines.

| 4m ↑

FAGACEAE

1 2 3 4 5 6 7 8 9 10 11 12

Quercus coccifera L.
Kermes oak

This is the most dominant species of oak and can last for a long time as a bush, taking various forms as a defense against grazing goats. In its tree form, it was once considered to constitute a separate species (*Q. calliprinos*). Kermococcus vermillio, a beetle with scales that produce a red colouring (known as crimson) develops on its leaves, which are small, spiny, and of a lighter colour on the underside. This gives the tree its name.

| 1-15m ↑ |

FAGACEAE

1 2 3 4 5 6 7 8 9 10 11 12

Quercus ilex L.
Holm oak

This is a beautiful, evergreen tree which can reach a height of 20 metres. Its leaves are up to 7cm in length and are leathery with a small stalk, elliptical-lanceolate with little or no toothing at the lips; the latter more or less differentiates them from the other species. The acorn cups are small and hemispherical, covering the acorns only up to the middle. The trees often form small forests. The *smilax* referred to by Theophrastus is probably the same tree.

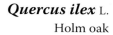 | 20m ↑ |

FAGACEAE

1 2 3 4 5 6 7 8 9 10 11 12

Quercus macrolepis KOTSCHY
Valonia oak

Quite a number of these trees are to be found on Crete. In particular, there are small forests to the south of the city of Rethymnon. The leaves have pointed lobes and the 'cups' have large scales, a characteristic which gives the tree its name. The galls contain tannins and for this reason were used in the past in the tanning process.

| 5-15m ↑ |

Quercus pubescens WILLD.
Downy oak

Also known as *Q. brachyphylla*, this oak has relatively small leaves, downy on the underside with rounded-off lobes. The galls have 'cups' with large scales. Loosely distributed over almost all of the island.

| 5-10m ↑ |

Blackstonia perfoliata (L.) HUDS.
Yellow-wort

As is apparent from the name, this little herbaceous plant is distinguished by its very characteristic fused leaves encircling a stem which branches at its tip. The basal leaves are concentrated in a rosette. The flowers are yellow with 7-8 lobes in a terminal umbel. Usually found on slopes.

| 10-30cm ↑ |

Centaurium erythraea RAFN
Common centaury

The spikes of numerous pink flowers do not permit this beautiful plant to go unnoticed. It has quadrangular stems, erect and much-branched, and unlobed leaves, the lower ones being larger and arranged in a rosette. The flowers have 5 petals which are joined at the base. In times past it was used as a febrifuge. Found in rocky locations, on slopes and roadsides.

| 10-50cm ↑ |

GENTIANACEAE

1 2 3 4 5 6 7 8 9 10 11 12

Centaurium maritimum Fritsch.
Yellow centary

A small, annual herbaceous plant with whitish-yellow flowers which distinguish it from the other species of centaury. The calyx has sharply-pointed lobes smaller than the corolla.
The leaves are ovate-lanceolate and stalkless. It prefers damp locations near the sea and the edges of streams. Despite its name, this plant is also found at higher altitudes; it is loosely distributed all over the island.

| 5-20cm ↑ |

GENTIANACEAE

1 2 3 4 5 6 7 8 9 10 11 12

Centaurium pulchellum (Sw.) Druce
Lesser centaury

This is a small, branching plant with ovate, opposite, stalkless leaves. The flowers are pink and arranged in loose inflorescences. Generally, it resembles *C. erythraea* but differs in size as well as in the absence of a leaf rosette at the base. Found in damp locations.

| 5-25cm ↑ |

GERANIACEAE

1 2 3 4 5 6 7 8 9 10 11 12

Erodium gruinum (L.) L'Her
Long-beaked heronsbill or storksbill

The erodia, like the geraniums which they resemble, took their name from the characteristic fruit with its long beak which recalls that of a heron. *E. gruinum* is an annual, hairy plant with three-lobed, toothed leaves. The flowers are on a very long flower-stalk, with violet petals which fall a few hours after blooming. Found in stony places.

| 20-40cm ↑ |

Geranium robertianum L.
Herb Robert

The fruits produced by this species of the genus resemble the beak of a crane in shape, hence its name. *G. robertianum* has trilobate leaves, each lobe itself divided into two, and small pink flowers. The plant which is often a russet shade, is very hairy.

| 10-30cm ↑ |

Geranium tuberosum L.
Tuberous cranesbill

A plant with a tuberous rhizome, whence it takes its name. It is a perennial, downy and with palm-like leaves with thin, deeply-divided lobes. The sepals are hairy and the petals 1 – 1.5cm, pink or violet, larger than the sepals. Found in fields and on roadsides.

| 10-40cm ↑ |

Globularia alypum L.
Shrubby globularia

An evergreen, densely-branched shrub with oblong-lanceolate leaves, entire or with a few shallow lobes, distributed along the whole length of the stem. The flower-bearing heads are hemispherical, with a diameter of up to 3cm and toothed florets, blue-violet in colour. This is an aromatic plant with purgative properties. Found in dry, stony areas, phrygana and thickets.

| 30-80cm ↑ |

GUTTIFERAE

1 2 3 4 5 6 7 8 9 10 11 12

Hypericum amblycalyx Coustur. & Gand. ●
Hypericum amblycalyx

This plant resembles *H. empetrifolium* but has whorls consisting of 4 leaves. It is endemic to eastern Crete and found along roadsides, on slopes, and in rocky places. *H. jovis*, also endemic, replaces it in the western part of the island.

 | 30-50cm ↑ |

GUTTIFERAE

1 2 3 4 5 6 7 8 9 10 11 12

Hypericum empetrifolium Willd.
Hypericum empetrifolium

The numerous, blindingly yellow flowers of this plant immediately distinguish it from the others. It has erect, russet-coloured stems and small, linear leaves which grow in tripartite whorls along the whole length of the stem. The petals are narrow, much longer than the sepals, and the stamens are in bunches, joined at the base. The plant is used in folk medicine as a healing agent. Found in thickets, on slopes, and in rocky locations.

| 30-50cm ↑ |

GUTTIFERAE

1 2 3 4 5 6 7 8 9 10 11 12

Hypericum empetrifolium ssp. *oliganthum* L. ●
Hypericum empetrifolium ssp. oliganthum

This is another endemic sub-species with consider-able resemblance to its parent species but with markedly fewer leaves, a characteristic which gave it its name. Found on rocky slopes, in phrygana, and in stony loca-tions.

| 20-60cm ↑ |

• *Hypericum empetrifolium* **ssp.** *tortuosum* (Rech.f.) Hageman   GUTTIFERAE

Hypericum empetrifolium ssp. tortuosum

| 1 | 2 | 3 | 4 | 5 | 6 | 7 | 8 | 9 | 10 | 11 | 12 |

A plant which is endemic to Crete and a subspecies of the widely distributed *H. empetrifolium*. It is a creeping plant with a woody stem and likes to grow from clefts in the rocks. It is found at altitudes above 1300m, in the three large mountain massifs of the island.

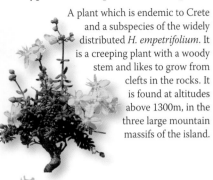

| 20-50cm →

• *Hypericum kelleri* Bald.   GUTTIFERAE

Hypericum kelleri

| 1 | 2 | 3 | 4 | 5 | 6 | 7 | 8 | 9 | 10 | 11 | 12 |

A small, creeping hypericum, endemic to the White Mountains. It resembles *H. trichocaulon* and is met just as frequently with 4 petals instead of 5, which are more often stippled and slightly toothed. Found on clay soil in little clumps, the plant has been characterized as endangered.

| 10-20cm →

Hypericum perfoliatum L.   GUTTIFERAE

Hypericum perfoliatum

| 1 | 2 | 3 | 4 | 5 | 6 | 7 | 8 | 9 | 10 | 11 | 12 |

A plant with an erect stem which has two characteristic lines along its length. The leaves are lanceolate, smooth and opposite, with transparent stippling; their length can reach 6cm and they are periblastic, a characteristic which gives the name to this species. The flowers are yellow and up to 2.5cm in size, and the sharply-pointed sepals have black stippling. The stamens are of about the same length as the petals. Found in ditches and shady places.

| 20-40cm ↑

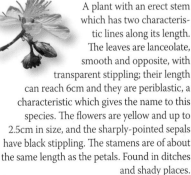

GUTTIFERAE

| 1 | 2 | 3 | 4 | 5 | 6 | 7 | 8 | 9 | 10 | 11 | 12 |

Hypericum perforatum L.
Perforate St. John's wort

This plant typically has black stippling on almost all its parts. It has an erect stem with two swollen lines along its length and elongated leaves, ovate and grey in colour, lighter on the underside. The leaves bear a multitude of transparent stipples which give them a perforated appearance – hence the name. The sepals are rather shorter than the petals. Found in fallow fields, dry and stony locations, and in phrygana.

| 10-50cm ↑ |

GUTTIFERAE

| 1 | 2 | 3 | 4 | 5 | 6 | 7 | 8 | 9 | 10 | 11 | 12 |

Hypericum trichocaulon Boiss. & Heldr. ●
Hypericum trichocaulon

A small, beautiful plant, endemic to the mountains of western Crete. It has many stems, erect or creeping, and elongated, ovate leaves with transparent black stippling. The flowers have petals that are deep red on the underside and sepals that are smaller, with black stippling. Found in stony locations, often in the shade of other plants.

| 5-15cm ↑ |

GUTTIFERAE

| 1 | 2 | 3 | 4 | 5 | 6 | 7 | 8 | 9 | 10 | 11 | 12 |

Hypericum triquetrifolium Turra
Hypericum triquetrifolium

A plant with many erect, branching stems. The leaves are periblastic, without glands, and are small, triangular, and opposite with a wavy lip. The yellow flowers do not have stippling and develop in a pyramid-shaped fan. Found in abandoned fields, on roadsides, and in coastal locations.

| 50-80cm ↑ |

Acinos alpinus (L.) MOENCH. / syn. *Satureja alpina*   LABIATAE
Acinos alpinus

| 1 | 2 | 3 | 4 | 5 | 6 | 7 | 8 | 9 | 10 | 11 | 12 |

A small, herbaceous plant with branching stems, erect or prostrate. The leaves are usually unlobed, ovate-lanceolate, downy and with a small stalk. The small, funnel-shaped pink flowers grow from the leaf axils and have an oblong, hairy calyx with characteristic stripes. Found in stony locations in the mountain and alpine zone.

| 10-30cm ↑ → |

Ballota pseudodictamnus BENTH.   LABIATAE
Ballota pseudodictamnus

| 1 | 2 | 3 | 4 | 5 | 6 | 7 | 8 | 9 | 10 | 11 | 12 |

Similar to B. acetabulosa but with leaves up to 2cm and very small flowers. Theophrastus refers to it as *díctamnon* but naturally it has nothing to do with the plant which is known under that name today. His 'pseudodíctamnon' refers not to this plant but to its relative, *B. acetabulosa*. Found in stony places.

| 20-50cm ↑ |

Calamintha cretica (L.) LAM. / συν. *Satureja cretica*   LABIATAE
Calamintha cretica

| 1 | 2 | 3 | 4 | 5 | 6 | 7 | 8 | 9 | 10 | 11 | 12 |

A phrygana plant, downy and with woody stems and ovate, very hairy leaves. The corolla is whitish-pink and larger than the calyx, which has sharply-pointed lobes. It is endemic and mainly found in the White Mountains.

10-40cm ↑ |

LABIATAE

| 1 | 2 | 3 | 4 | 5 | 6 | 7 | 8 | 9 | 10 | 11 | 12 |

Lamium amplexicaule L.
Henbit deadnettle

A delicate annual plant, downy with an erect stem and toothed, kidney-shaped leaves, the upper ones periblastic and overlapping or joined, the lower ones on a long stalk. The flowers are whitish-pink with a thin tube that is much longer than the calyx. The plant is common in both cultivated and fallow fields.

| 10-30cm ↑ |

LABIATAE

| 1 | 2 | 3 | 4 | 5 | 6 | 7 | 8 | 9 | 10 | 11 | 12 |

Lamium garganicum L.
Large red deadnettle

A perennial plant, much-branched; it can take the form of a bush. The leaves are heart-shaped, toothed and have a long stalk. The flowers are numerous with a tube much longer than the calyx; they are white, with pink linear markings and stipples. The upper lip is irregularly toothed, with a length the same as that of the tube. Found in the mountain and alpine zone, often beneath other plants.

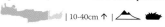

| 10-40cm ↑ |

LABIATAE

| 1 | 2 | 3 | 4 | 5 | 6 | 7 | 8 | 9 | 10 | 11 | 12 |

Lavandula stoechas L.
French lavender

The wild lavender is a much-branched phrygano plant, very aromatic with downy, linear leaves along the length of the stem. The flowers are small, funnel-shaped and dark violet in colour, arranged in a dense ear-like spike at the tip of which large rosy bracts develop, with a length of up to 5cm. Found in thickets, phrygana and in stony locations.

| 30-100cm ↑ |

Mentha pulegium L.
Pennyroyal

1 2 3 4 5 6 7 8 9 10 11 12

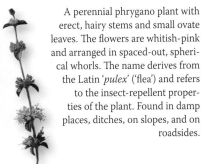

A perennial phrygano plant with erect, hairy stems and small ovate leaves. The flowers are whitish-pink and arranged in spaced-out, spherical whorls. The name derives from the Latin '*pulex*' ('flea') and refers to the insect-repellent properties of the plant. Found in damp places, ditches, on slopes, and on roadsides.

| 20-50cm ↑ |

Nepeta melissifolia LAM.
Nepeta melissifolia

1 2 3 4 5 6 7 8 9 10 11 12

A perennial plant with an erect, downy stem; the leaves have long stalks and are almost triangular, toothed and similar to those of the genus Melissa. The flowers are blue or violet with dark stippling and the calyx is short with stripes which reach to the middle of the tube. The flowers develop in whorls which all together form a loose, cone-like spike. Found in phrygana and in gorges.

| 20-50cm ↑ |

Nepeta scordotis L. / syn. *Nepeta hirsuta*
Nepeta scordotis

1 2 3 4 5 6 7 8 9 10 11 12

A very hairy plant, greyish-green, with erect branching stems and large, thick, ovate to heart-shaped leaves which are lightly toothed, stalked and have a relief blazon. The flowers are small and white, in spike-like alternate whorls. Found in phrygana, stony places, and fields.

| 30-80cm ↑ |

LABIATAE

`1` `2` `3` `4` `5` `6` `7` `8` `9` `10` `11` `12`

Origanum dictamnus L. ●
Cretan dittany

The fame of this little phrygano plant, which is endemic to Crete, assumed mythological proportions from antiquity onwards. Even today, dittany is considered to be a panacea for a number of ailments. It is a much-branched plant with ovate leaves, covered in dense white down. The flowers are whitish-pink with many russet-coloured, overlapping bracts. Found on cliffs, in gorges and in rocky locations.

| 5-40cm ↑ |

LABIATAE

`1` `2` `3` `4` `5` `6` `7` `8` `9` `10` `11` `12`

Origanum microphyllum (BENTH.) VOGEL ●
Origanum microphyllum

A small, much-branched phrygano plant with the aroma of lavender. It has thin, russet-coloured stems and little ovate, downy leaves. The flowers are small and pinkish-violet, arranged in a small ear-like spike, with bracts covered with dense white hairs. Found on stony slopes and in phrygana in the White Mountains of Crete, and on Dikti.

| 1030cm ↑ |

LABIATAE

`1` `2` `3` `4` `5` `6` `7` `8` `9` `10` `11` `12`

Origanum onites L.
Pot marjoram

This phrygano plant has erect stems and downy, heart-shaped opposite leaves along the whole length of the stem; the lower ones are stalked, the upper ones stalkless. The flowers are white with large stamens in dense corymbs. The plant is one form of common oregano which is collected along with the other more or less similar form (*O. vulgare*) and used as a herb in cooking. Found in stony places and on slopes.

| 20-40cm ↑ |

Phlomis cretica C.Presl.
Phlomis cretica

| 1 | 2 | 3 | 4 | 5 | 6 | 7 | 8 | 9 | 10 | 11 | 12 |

A downy, much-branched phrygano plant which does not exceed 50cm in height. The leaves are lanceolate with a velvet surface; the lower ones have longer leaf-stalks than the upper ones. The flowers are yellow, longer than the toothed and hairy calyces, in dense whorls. Found in dry, stony locations and phrygana.

| 30-60cm ↑ |

Phlomis fruticosa L.
Jerusalem sage

| 1 | 2 | 3 | 4 | 5 | 6 | 7 | 8 | 9 | 10 | 11 | 12 |

A branching phrygano plant or shrub, similar to P. cretica but with a height which can reach to over 1 metre and leaves that are white on the underside, the lower ones stalked, the upper ones stalkless. The flowers are yellow, up to 4cm, with the upper lobe hairy, ar- ranged in alternate whorls. Found in rocky places, in thickets and in phrygana.

| 50-1,20cm ↑ |

Phlomis lanata Willd.
Phlomis lanata

| 1 | 2 | 3 | 4 | 5 | 6 | 7 | 8 | 9 | 10 | 11 | 12 |

A phrygano plant, endemic to Crete, which somewhat resembles *P. cretica* but is easily differentiated by its ovate, almost round leaves and its denser hairs. The flowers are small, up to 2cm. Found in rocky places, in thickets, in phrygana and in glades.

| 30-50cm ↑ |

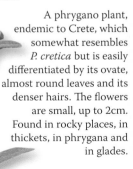

LABIATAE

| 1 | 2 | 3 | 4 | 5 | 6 | 7 | 8 | 9 | 10 | 11 | 12 |

Prasium majus L.
Prasium

A perennial phrygano plant or small shrub with smooth, woody stems. The leaves are heart-shaped, smooth, toothed and grassy green in colour, with a little stalk. It is identified by its white flowers which are always in pairs, with bell-shaped calyces which are hairy on the inside. P. majus is a basic component of *hórta* – the mixture of wild greens which is known as *tsitsiristá*, used as a filling in *hortópites* (little pastry envelopes) or served as an accompaniment to meat dishes. It is usually found on rocky slopes.

| 20-80cm ↑ |

LABIATAE

| 1 | 2 | 3 | 4 | 5 | 6 | 7 | 8 | 9 | 10 | 11 | 12 |

Prunella cretensis GAND. ●
Prunella cretensis

A small, hairy, perennial herbaceous plant with sphenoid, toothed leaves. The flowers are whitish-pink in a dense terminal spike. It is endemic and found in stony locations in the mountain zone. P. laciniata is similar in appearance, but has whitish-yellow flow-ers and prefers lower altitudes.

| 5-15cm ↑ |

LABIATAE

| 1 | 2 | 3 | 4 | 5 | 6 | 7 | 8 | 9 | 10 | 11 | 12 |

Rosmarinus officinalis L.
Rosemary

A large, much-branched phrygano plant or bush with narrow, spiky leaves. Axillary flow-ers, white or blue, with characteristically large stamens. The plant is strongly aromatic and has may uses in the manufacture of pharmaceuticals and perfumes. The leaves are used as a herb in cookery. Rosemary is usually culti-vated or self-sowing near to settlements.

| 50-150cm ↑ |

Salvia pomifera L.

Salvia pomifera

LABIATAE

| 1 | 2 | 3 | 4 | 5 | 6 | 7 | 8 | 9 | 10 | 11 | 12 |

A phrygano plant with slightly less down than S. argentea and with large wavy leaves, thinly toothed at the lip. The corolla is whitish-pink and in dense racemes, with calyces that are bell-shaped and continue to grow after the flowers have withered. This is a very aromatic plant which is often used as a tisane (tea). Found on rocky cliffs and slopes.

|60- 120cm ↑ |

Salvia triloba L. / syn. *Salvia fruticosa*

Three-lobed sage

LABIATAE

| 1 | 2 | 3 | 4 | 5 | 6 | 7 | 8 | 9 | 10 | 11 | 12 |

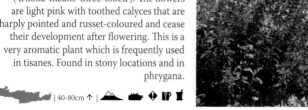

A perennial phrygano plant with many stems, erect and covered with dense white down, sticky at the tip. The leaves are green on the surface and whitish on the underside with two small lobe-like leaflets at the base, a characteristic which gives the plant its name ('triloba' means 'three-lobed'). The flowers are light pink with toothed calyces that are sharply pointed and russet-coloured and cease their development after flowering. This is a very aromatic plant which is frequently used in tisanes. Found in stony locations and in phrygana.

| 40-80cm ↑ |

Salvia verbenaca L.

Wild clary

LABIATAE

| 1 | 2 | 3 | 4 | 5 | 6 | 7 | 8 | 9 | 10 | 11 | 12 |

This is a perennial with a thin stem, markedly quadrangular, and slightly hairy. The leaves are large and wing-lobed; those at the base have a long stalk, and those on the stem are stalkless. The flowers are bluish-violet, in loosely arranged whorls along the whole length of the stem. Small plants are often observed with densely arranged whorls. Found on roadsides and in stony locations.

| 30-60cm ↑ |

LABIATAE

| 1 | 2 | 3 | 4 | 5 | 6 | 7 | 8 | 9 | 10 | 11 | 12 |

Salvia viridis L.
Red-topped sage

An annual with an erect stem and leaves that are ovate, stalked, slightly toothed and grass-green in colour. The flowers have a large upper lip and are violet-coloured and arranged in loose whorls. The calyces continue to grow larger after flowering. Found in phrygana and stony places.

| 10-40cm ↑ |

LABIATAE

| 1 | 2 | 3 | 4 | 5 | 6 | 7 | 8 | 9 | 10 | 11 | 12 |

Satureja spinosa L.
Satureja spinosa

This is a phrygano plant of the mountain and alpine zone and often forms beautiful heads on the rocks. It has many branching, spiny stems and small, lanceolate leaves. The flowers are white and axillary. It is endemic to the south-east Aegean and found in the three large mountain massifs of Crete.

| 10-30cm ↑ |

LABIATAE

| 1 | 2 | 3 | 4 | 5 | 6 | 7 | 8 | 9 | 10 | 11 | 12 |

Satureja thymbra L.
Summer savory

This is a small phrygano plant, much-branched and loosely covered with white hairs, with a scent similar to that of thyme. It has inverted ovate leaves, pointed and with 'eyelashes' near the base. The flowers are light pink and arranged in whorls with calyces that are pointed and hairy. A very aromatic plant which is often used as a flavouring in meat dishes. Found in dry, stony locations and in phrygana.

| 10-30cm ↑ |

● *Scutellaria hirta* Sm.
Scutellaria hirta

| 1 | 2 | 3 | 4 | 5 | 6 | 7 | 8 | 9 | 10 | 11 | 12 |

A small, very hairy plant with ovate to heart-shaped leaves, slightly saw-edged. The flowers are whitish-pink and drooping, in dense inflorescences. The calyces are pink, and very characteristic. The plant is endemic to Crete and found in crevices in the rocks at high altitudes.

| 10-20cm ↑ → | ▲ ⚓ ◆

● *Scutellaria sieberi* Benth.
Scutellaria sieberi

| 1 | 2 | 3 | 4 | 5 | 6 | 7 | 8 | 9 | 10 | 11 | 12 |

A grass-green plant with long, erect or nodding stems and ovate, lightly toothed leaves. The flowers are usually white in an elongated spike. The whole plant is covered with dense down. It is endemic to Crete and usually prefers rocky slopes.

| 30-50cm ↑ → | ▲ ⬛

● *Sideritis syriaca* ssp. *syriaca* L.
Sideritis syriaca ssp. syriaca

| 1 | 2 | 3 | 4 | 5 | 6 | 7 | 8 | 9 | 10 | 11 | 12 |

Despite the name, this plant is endemic to Crete. It is very downy with an erect stem and lanceolate leaves, the lower ones stalked and the upper ones stalkless. The flowers are yellow, arranged in whorls in a loose order. The plant is used as a tisane (mountain tea) and is abundant in the Madares – the mountain wilderness of the White Mountains.

| 20-60cm ↑ | ▲ ⬛ 🌿 🍵

| 1 | 2 | 3 | 4 | 5 | 6 | 7 | 8 | 9 | 10 | 11 | 12 |

Stachys cretica L.
Mediterranean woundwort

A perennial, whitish-green coloured herbaceous plant with numerous strong stems, erect
and covered with dense
white hairs. The leaves are
elongated, lanceolate and
finely toothed, the lower
ones stalked, the upper ones almost
stalkless. The flowers are light pink and
arranged in whorls at a fair distance from
each other. Found in stony locations,
phrygana, and on roadsides.

| 20-70cm ↑ |

| 1 | 2 | 3 | 4 | 5 | 6 | 7 | 8 | 9 | 10 | 11 | 12 |

Stachys spinosa L. ●
Spiny woundwort

This endemic, strongly spined
phrygano plant has numerous
much-branched and
hairy stems and usually
grows in a spherical shape.
The leaves are elongated,
downy, concave, and
almost stalkless.
The flowers are white or
pink, often occurring singly
with a toothed, sharply-
pointed calyx. Found in phrygana, on slopes,
and in rocky locations.

| 20-60cm ↑ |

| 1 | 2 | 3 | 4 | 5 | 6 | 7 | 8 | 9 | 10 | 11 | 12 |

Teucrium alpestre Sm. ●
Teucrium alpestre

A low, spreading phrygano plant with small,
ovate leaves. The flower has 5 lobes and is
of a delicate whitish-yellow colour. Despite
its name, it is met at both alpine and lower
altitudes in exposed stony locations and
phrygana.

| 20-50cm → |

Teucrium divaricatum Sieber ex Heldr. / syn. *T. graecum*   LABIATAE
Teucrium divaricatum

A perennial, branched phrygano plant with woody, delicately haired stems and ovate leaves that are toothed and have a wedge-shaped base. The calyx is reddish-brown, tubular, toothed and hairy. The flowers are pink with a hairy tube longer than the calyx. Particularly characteristic are the large stamens, and the strongly folded middle lobe of the lower lip. Found in rocky locations and on slopes.

| 20-50cm ↑ |

Thymus capitatus (L.) Hoff. & Link. / syn. *Coridothymus capitatus*   LABIATAE
Thymus capitatus

This is the most common but at the same time most important of all the thymes, since it is responsible for the production of the best honey in the world. It forms small, much-branched and head-shaped bushes, which during the flowering period are bathed in pink, due to the flowers which form cone-shaped heads. The very large stamens are typical, as are the 'eyelashes' at the bases of the leaves. Found in dry, stony locations and in phrygana.

| 10-30cm ↑ |

Thymus leucotrichus Halácsy   LABIATAE
Thymus leucotrichus

A small plant, covered in white hairs – hence its name. The leaves are lanceolate and the flowers whitish–pink, arranged in small heads. A very beautiful plant which prefers stony locations and crevices in the rocks of the mountain and alpine zone.

| 10-20cm ↑ |

LAURACEAE

`1` `2` `3` `4` `5` `6` `7` `8` `9` `10` `11` `12`

Laurus nobilis L.
Sweet bay

The plant occurs normally in bush form, but very often becomes a tree which can reach a good height. The leaves are distinguished by their numerous aromatic oil-bearing glands from which bay tree oil is distilled, to be used for pharmaceutical purposes and in perfumery. The symbolism of the bay tree is manifold; even today its branches are used for garlands and decoration at festivals.

| 5m ↑ |

LEGUMINOSAE

`1` `2` `3` `4` `5` `6` `7` `8` `9` `10` `11` `12`

Anagyris foetida L.
Bean trefoil

A shrub or tree which emits a strong, rank odour when shaken. The leaves are stalked and consist of three stalkless leaflets. The flowers are yellow in axillary racemes, with calyces which are bell-shaped and toothed. The main (standard) petal is smaller than the elongated wings with black spots on its internal surface. Found in ditches, along hedges, and in thickets.

| 1-4m ↑ |

LEGUMINOSAE

Anthyllis tetraphylla L. / syn. *Tripodion tetraphyllum*

`1` `2` `3` `4` `5` `6` `7` `8` `9` `10` `11` `12`

Bladder vetch

An annual, normally creeping herbaceous plant with leaves consisting of 3-5 leaflets, that of the tip being much larger than the others. The flowers grow in the leaf axils with a whitish-yellow main (standard) petal, larger than the yellow wings. The calyx is downy, swollen and yellow-green with russet stripes. Found at the edges of fields and in phrygana.

| 10-40cm → |

Anthyllis vulneraria L.
Kidney vetch

LEGUMINOSAE

1	2	3	4	5	6	7	8	9	10	11	12

A hairy, erect or creeping herbaceous plant with polymorphic leaves. The lower leaves consist of unevenly-sized leaflets with the central one much larger, while the upper leaves are more or less of the same size. The flowers are whitish-pink with the heads surrounded by leaf-like bracts and swollen calyces, which are very hairy. A polymorphic plant with many sub-species, and considered to have healing properties - hence its name. It is common in fields and on roadsides.

| 20-60cm ↑ |

Astragalus angustifolius Lam.
Astragalus angustifolius

LEGUMINOSAE

1	2	3	4	5	6	7	8	9	10	11	12

A spiny phrygano plant which grows in beautiful semicircular masses. The formation of some bushes into this shape is not a matter of chance. The spiny stems, intricately branching, protect the plant from grazing animals, wind and snow, while retaining shade and moisture through the summer period. The flower is white with a large standard petal, and wings and a keel which are much smaller, the latter with violet shading. Found in stony locations in the mountain and alpine zone.

| 20-60cm ↑ |

● *Astragalus creticus* Lam./ syn. *Astracantha cretica*
Astragalus creticus

LEGUMINOSAE

1	2	3	4	5	6	7	8	9	10	11	12

A dense, much-branching shrub, very spiny and with leaves which consist of 5-6 pairs of downy, lanceolate leaflets with a strong spine in the middle. The flowers are axillary, whitish-pink in colour. The plant forms impressive pillow-like bushes and is found in the mountain and alpine zone; it is, however, absent from the White Mountains.

| 20-50cm ↑ |

LEGUMINOSAE

| 1 | 2 | 3 | 4 | 5 | 6 | 7 | 8 | 9 | 10 | 11 | 12 |

Calicotome villosa (Poir.) Link
Spiny broom

A common sight in the Greek countryside – the brilliant yellow slopes
covered in broom and bathed in
the scent of this beautiful plant.
It is branching, very spiny and
downy, with typical grooves along the
length of the stems. The leaves have
ovate leaflets, downy on the underside. The flowers are yellow, often in
groups in the axils of the branches.
Found in hedges, in thickets and in
phrygana.

| 0,50-2m ↑ |

LEGUMINOSAE

| 1 | 2 | 3 | 4 | 5 | 6 | 7 | 8 | 9 | 10 | 11 | 12 |

Ceratonia siliqua C.
Carob or locust tree

This beautiful tree was cultivated
in bygone days for its fruits, the
well-known carobs, whose seeds
were once used (although not as
much today) in the production of cel-
lulose and the pod for the production
of an aerated beverage or for animal feed.
The size of the seed is always the same and
was used to define a unit of weight for gold
– the 'carat'. The flowers are very small and
develop in long racemes. The leaves have ovate
leaflets, and are smooth and leathery.

| 3-10m ↑ |

LEGUMINOSAE

| 1 | 2 | 3 | 4 | 5 | 6 | 7 | 8 | 9 | 10 | 11 | 12 |

Cercis siliquastrum L.
Judas tree

This beautiful tree with very decorative flowers is connected with Judas;
according to tradition, he was
hanged on such a tree after the
betrayal. The flowers, like the
calyx, are pink and develop in
racemes directly from the branches.
The smooth, kidney-shaped leaves
follow the flowering and, when
the hanging pods appear, take on
a dull appearance. It is often cultivated as a decorative plant.

| 2-5m ↑ |

Cicer incisum K. Malý

Cicer incisum

LEGUMINOSAE

| 1 | 2 | 3 | 4 | 5 | 6 | 7 | 8 | 9 | 10 | 11 | 12 |

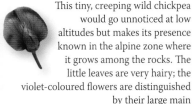

This tiny, creeping wild chickpea would go unnoticed at low altitudes but makes its presence known in the alpine zone where it grows among the rocks. The little leaves are very hairy; the violet-coloured flowers are distinguished by their large main (standard) petal.

| 5-10cm ↑ →

Coronilla parviflora Willd. / syn. *Securigera parviflora*   LEGUMINOSAE

Coronilla parviflora

| 1 | 2 | 3 | 4 | 5 | 6 | 7 | 8 | 9 | 10 | 11 | 12 |

This little coronilla has long, slender stems and leaves surrounded by sphenoid leaflets. The plant is found with pink or yellow flowers, 5-8 in an umbel. Found in olive groves, phrygana, and stony places.

| 10-30cm ↑

● *Coronilla globosa* Lam. / syn. *Securigera globosa*   LEGUMINOSAE

Coronilla globosa

| 1 | 2 | 3 | 4 | 5 | 6 | 7 | 8 | 9 | 10 | 11 | 12 |

A perennial shrub, endemic to Crete. The leaves have more than 10 ovate, elongated and smooth leaflets. The flowers are numerous and arranged in spherical heads with a diameter of up to 6cm. The petals are white, the main (standard) petal with pink veining, the keel with pink shading. Found on the sides of gorges, on slopes and in cool, shady locations.

| 1-1,5m ↑

LEGUMINOSAE

| 1 | 2 | 3 | 4 | 5 | 6 | 7 | 8 | 9 | 10 | 11 | 12 |

Ebenus cretica L. ●
Cretan ebony

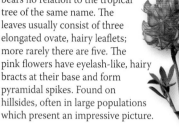

Despite its name, this impressive shrub which is only found on Crete bears no relation to the tropical tree of the same name. The leaves usually consist of three elongated ovate, hairy leaflets; more rarely there are five. The pink flowers have eyelash-like, hairy bracts at their base and form pyramidal spikes. Found on hillsides, often in large populations which present an impressive picture.

| 50-100cm ↑ |

LEGUMINOSAE

| 1 | 2 | 3 | 4 | 5 | 6 | 7 | 8 | 9 | 10 | 11 | 12 |

Genista acanthoclada DC.
Genista acanthoclada

A much-branching, cushion-shaped shrub with wand-like stems, very spiny, hence the name acanthoclada derived from the Greek words *ákantha* (spine) and *kládos* (branch). The leaves are small and stalkless, consisting of three lanceolate, elongated leaflets, which develop at the points where the stems branch. There are racemes of slightly downy flowers at the ends of the stems. Found in thickets, in phrygana and in downgraded areas.

| 0,30-1,50m ↑ |

LEGUMINOSAE

| 1 | 2 | 3 | 4 | 5 | 6 | 7 | 8 | 9 | 10 | 11 | 12 |

Lathyrus clymenum L.
Lathrys clymenum

An annual plant, climbing and with a very characteristic winged stem. The leaves have elongated-lanceolate florets. A branching tendril develops at the tip of the upper leaves. The flowers have a purple main petal and pink wings. Found in olive groves and fields.

| 30-80cm ↑ → |

Lotus cytisoides L.
Lotus cytisoides

| 1 | 2 | 3 | 4 | 5 | 6 | 7 | 8 | 9 | 10 | 11 | 12 |

This little annual plant, which likes coastal rocks and sands, has erect or spreading stems and leaves with sphenoid leaflets. The flowers are yellow and arranged (2-6) in a hemispherical inflorescence. Like the other species of the genus, it bears absolutely no relation to the 'lotus' of antiquity, which is of the species *Zizyphus lotus*.

| 10-30cm ↑ → | ◭ ⌂ ⚓

Lupinus albus L.
White lupin

| 1 | 2 | 3 | 4 | 5 | 6 | 7 | 8 | 9 | 10 | 11 | 12 |

The lupins are edible and even today their yellow fruits are found on every dinner table during the Lenten period of fasting. *L. albus* is an annual plant; its leaves, like those of all the lupins, are arranged in a ray-like order, elliptic and hairy on the underside. The flowers are white with a short flower-stalk, alternate or in pairs in short racemes. The calyces have lips of equal length. The lupin is self-sowing near areas where it is already being grown.

| 50-100cm ↑ | ◭ ⚓ 🌿

Lupinus angustifolius L.
Narrow-leaved lupin

| 1 | 2 | 3 | 4 | 5 | 6 | 7 | 8 | 9 | 10 | 11 | 12 |

An annual plant, erect and with leaves that have 5-9 characteristic, narrow leaflets, hairy on the underside. The flowers are a beautiful blue in colour, alternate, with short flower-stalks and in a long raceme. The lower lip of the calyx is larger than the upper one, which is deeply bilobate. Found in phrygana, in thickets and in fields.

| 20-60cm ↑ | ◭ ⚓

LEGUMINOSAE

| 1 | 2 | 3 | 4 | 5 | 6 | 7 | 8 | 9 | 10 | 11 | 12 |

Lupinus pilosus L.
Lupinus pilosus

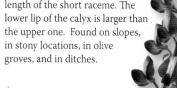

An annual plant, hairy and erect. The leaves have 7-11 oblong-lanceolate leaflets which are hairy on both sides. The flowers are blue with white brush-strokes and arranged in whorls along the whole length of the short raceme. The lower lip of the calyx is larger than the upper one. Found on slopes, in stony locations, in olive groves, and in ditches.

| 10-40cm ↑ |

LEGUMINOSAE

| 1 | 2 | 3 | 4 | 5 | 6 | 7 | 8 | 9 | 10 | 11 | 12 |

Medicago arborea L.
Tree medick

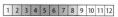

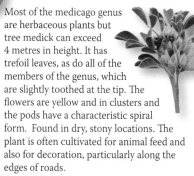

Most of the medicago genus are herbaceous plants but tree medick can exceed 4 metres in height. It has trefoil leaves, as do all of the members of the genus, which are slightly toothed at the tip. The flowers are yellow and in clusters and the pods have a characteristic spiral form. Found in dry, stony locations. The plant is often cultivated for animal feed and also for decoration, particularly along the edges of roads.

| 1-4m ↑ |

LEGUMINOSAE

| 1 | 2 | 3 | 4 | 5 | 6 | 7 | 8 | 9 | 10 | 11 | 12 |

Medicago marina L.
Sea medick

A perennial, creeping plant, covered in dense silver hairs. The leaves have three leaflets, wedge-shaped and very hairy. The flowers are yellow with the standard petal larger than the keel, in little racemes. The pods are spiral in shape with two or three twists. The plant prefers sandy locations near the sea, where it forms little thickets.

| 10-50cm ↑ → |

Medicago strasseri Greuter, Matthäs & Risse LEGUMINOSAE

Medicago strasseri

1 2 3 4 5 6 7 8 9 10 11 12

A shrub or small tree generally resembling *M. arborea* but with smaller flowers and leaves. The plant was only recently identified (in 1982) and is endemic to Crete. It is found on vertical rocky slopes of gorges in the northern part of the island.

| 50-150cm ↑ |

Onobrychis sphaciotica Greuter LEGUMINOSAE

Onobrychis sphaciotica

1 2 3 4 5 6 7 8 9 10 11 12

Like many of the psychanths, onobrychis attracts animals and the name of the genus describes how the donkey reacts by braying at the sight of the plant. *O. sphaciotica* is a beautiful plant with pink flowers which finds refuge on the rocky slopes. It is one of the rarest plants in Greece with a very limited distribution in the White Mountains. It is included in the Red Data Book and characterized as vulnerable.

| 30-80cm ↑ |

Ononis reclinata L. LEGUMINOSAE

Ononis reclinata

1 2 3 4 5 6 7 8 9 10 11 12

A small, hairy phrygano plant with erect or spreading stems and leaves with sphenoid leaflets, toothed at the tip. The flowers have a main petal which is whitish-pink with dark veining; the wings and keel are white. The plant prefers locations near the sea.

| 5-15cm ↑ |

LEGUMINOSAE

`1 2 3 4 5 6 7 8 9 10 11 12`

Ononis spinosa L. ●
Restharrow

A branching, phrygano plant with many spiny stems and leaves with ovate, toothed leaflets. The flowers are whitish–pink and larger than 1.5cm, with the standard petal larger than the keel. The calyx is hairy, toothed, and has pointed tips. Found in stony locations.

| 10-80cm ↑

LEGUMINOSAE

`1 2 3 4 5 6 7 8 9 10 11 12`

Psoralea bituminosa L. / syn. *Bituminaria bitominosa*
Bitumen pea

A polymorphic plant which oftern forms dense stands along the sides of roads. The stem is slender, erect and has leaves with three elongated, lanceolate and long-stalked leaflets. The flowers are blue-violet with hairy calyces in almost round heads which have a very long flower stalk and grow in the axils of the leaves. The plant is easily recognised by the characteristic smell of tar which it emits. Common on roadsides, in ditches and in fallow fields.

| 0,20 - 1m ↑

LEGUMINOSAE

`1 2 3 4 5 6 7 8 9 10 11 12`

Spartium junceum L.
Spanish broom

This shrub, which often embellishes the roadsides with its pleasantly-scented yellow flowers, has many long, thin stems and a few small, insignificant leaves. The flowers are arranged in racemes at the ends of the stems and produce flat pods up to 8cm in length. The strong, pliable stems of the plant are still used today to produce brooms and rope. Often cultivated as a decorative plant along the sides of roads.

| 1-3m ↑

Tetragonolobus purpureus Moench.
Winged pea, asparagus pea

LEGUMINOSAE

| 1 | 2 | 3 | 4 | 5 | 6 | 7 | 8 | 9 | 10 | 11 | 12 |

A small, hairy annual with broad, rhomboid leaflets. The flowers are solitary or in pairs, purple in colour, and axillary, with the wings longer than the main petal. Found in olive groves, fields, barren places, and ditches.

| 10-30cm ↑ |

Trifolium campestre Schreb.
Hop trefoil

LEGUMINOSAE

| 1 | 2 | 3 | 4 | 5 | 6 | 7 | 8 | 9 | 10 | 11 | 12 |

The clovers or trefoils take their name from their leaves which consist of three leaflets. They are small, herbaceous plants with butterfly-shaped flowers in heads or spikes. *T. campestre* is one of the few trefoils with many, small gold-yellow flowers in characteristic round heads which have a diameter a little larger than 1cm; the flowers take on a coffee-colour as time progresses. Found along roadsides, in ditches, olive groves, and in stony locations.

| 5-30cm ↑ |

Trifolium repens L.
White clover

LEGUMINOSAE

| 1 | 2 | 3 | 4 | 5 | 6 | 7 | 8 | 9 | 10 | 11 | 12 |

A perennial, usually creeping, and hairless. The leaflets have a very short stalk, and are elliptic in shape with a circular white blazon at the base and dark, irregular lines along the length of the central vein. The flower-bearing heads have long flower-stalks with flowers of up to 1cm, whitish-pink in colour. Found in fields, cool locations and in phrygana.

| 10-30cm → |

LEGUMINOSAE

| 1 | 2 | 3 | 4 | 5 | 6 | 7 | 8 | 9 | 10 | 11 | 12 |

Trifolium stellatum L.
Star clover

An annual plant, hairy and with leaflets that
are inverse heart-shaped, the
side leaflets almost white,
with veins and edges that
are grassy green. The
flower-bearing heads
are spherical on long
flower-stalks, and the flowers are white with yellow
or pinkish tones. The caly-
ces are hairy, and red on ripening when they
take a characteristic star-shaped form. Found
in fields, stony locations, and in phrygana.

| 10-30cm ↑ |

LEGUMINOSAE

| 1 | 2 | 3 | 4 | 5 | 6 | 7 | 8 | 9 | 10 | 11 | 12 |

Trifolium uniflorum L.
Trifolium uniflorum

A beautiful, perennial, usually with
a creeping habit, and leaves on
long stalks. The leaflets are
toothed, often with a white
blazon. The flowers are white
or whitish-pink, solitary and
on long flower-stalks which
grow in the axils of the lower
leaves. The calyx is tubular. Found in phrygana,
on slopes, and in dry,
stony locations.

| 10-20cm ↑ → |

LEGUMINOSAE

| 1 | 2 | 3 | 4 | 5 | 6 | 7 | 8 | 9 | 10 | 11 | 12 |

Trigonella balansae Boiss. & Reut.
Trigonella balansae

An annual with characteristic
leaves consisting of three
inverse-ovate, toothed leaflets. The flowers are yellow
in a globose, axillary raceme.
Usually found near the sea in
rocky and sandy locations.

| 20-40cm ↑ |

Vicia cretica Boiss. & Heldr.
Cretan vetch

An annual with leaves consisting of 3-5 pairs of lanceolate leaflets. The flowers are up to 1.5cm in size, with a red or pink main petal and white or whitish-pink wings. The calyx is much shorter than the corolla. Found in stony locations, often amidst spiny phrygana.

| 10-50cm ↑ → | ⛰ ⚓

Vicia tenuifolia Roth.
Vicia tenuifolia

A perennial plant, erect and with leaves consisting of 8-12 pairs of slender, linear leaflets. Numerous light-coloured flowers, pink or violet and nodding. Found on the Omalos and Katré plateaus in the White Mountains. The more distributed *V. villosa* (fodder vetch) is similar but has darker coloured flowers and broader leaves.

| 20-80cm ↑ | ⛰ ⚓

Linum arboreum L.
Tree flax

This is a small shrub with a woody stem and fleshy leaves. The basal leaves develop into a rosette and are spatulate with a length of up to 3cm, while the upper leaves are smaller and lanceolate. The flowers have 5 petals up to 3cm in length, much longer than the sepals, and are arranged in terminal racemes. It is normally found on the rocky slopes of gorges.

| 20-40cm ↑ | ⛰ ◆

LINACEAE

1 2 3 4 5 6 7 8 9 10 11 12

Linum bienne MILL. / syn. *Linum angustifolium*
Pale flax

A plant of slender growth, with many erect stems and narrow leaves that are lanceolate and alternate along the whole length of the stem. The flowers are light-coloured, blue-violet with dark veins, and the sepals smaller and spiky. The plant resembles *L. usitatissimum*, the cultivated flax which is much larger in size. Found in fields, phrygana, and olive groves.

| 20-50cm ↑ |

LORANTHACEAE

1 2 3 4 5 6 7 8 9 10 11 12

Viscum album L.
Mistletoe

An evergreen parasite with a preference for trees and in particular chestnut, pine and fir. The fruit is a round white berry whose sticky flesh was used in bygone days to make bird-lime, i.e to coat twigs used to entrap birds. The plant has had pharmaceutical uses since antiquity; Theophrastus believed it to be a remedy for epilepsy. The sticky fruit – the 'gue' of the Anglo-Saxons, is still used to decorate the doorways of houses at Christmas; this custom is a remnant of Druidic belief, while in Greek mythology Persephone used the plant to open the gates of Hades.

| 20-50cm ↑→ |

LYTHRACEAE

1 2 3 4 5 6 7 8 9 10 11 12

Lythrum junceum BANKS & SOL.
Lythrum junceum

A perennial plant with erect quadrangular stems. The leaves are elongated, stalkless, the lower ones opposite, the upper ones alternate and more densely arranged. The flowers are pink with a light-coloured throat, growing singly in the leaf axils. It is common along streams, the banks of rivers and in damp locations generally, often in dense stands.

| 20-70cm ↑ |

Alcea pallida (Willd.) Waldst. & Kit.

Alcea pallida

| 1 | 2 | 3 | 4 | 5 | 6 | 7 | 8 | 9 | 10 | 11 | 12 |

An impressive plant with a strong stem, erect and with a height that can exceed 2 metres. The leaves are large, hairy, and kidney-shaped with shallow lobes. The flowers are up to 8cm, pink or purple with a very short flower-stalk. The plant is common in hedges and on the sides of roads.

 | 1-2.5m ↑ |

Lavatera bryoniifolia Mill.

Lavatera bryoniifolia

| 1 | 2 | 3 | 4 | 5 | 6 | 7 | 8 | 9 | 10 | 11 | 12 |

A plant with many slender, tall branches. The leaves are palmately lobed, hairy and stalked, similar to those of the bryony, whence it takes its name. The flowers are pink with a diameter that can reach 4cm and in a loose arrangement, along almost the whole length of the stem. Normally found on roadsides and in dry locations.

| 1-2m ↑ |

Lavatera cretica L.

Cretan mallow, Small tree mallow

| 1 | 2 | 3 | 4 | 5 | 6 | 7 | 8 | 9 | 10 | 11 | 12 |

A smaller plant than L. bryonifolia, with erect or spreading stems. The leaves are downy, the upper ones with five deep, toothed lobes, and the lower ones almost round. The flowers are pink with dark veining and grow in bunches in the leaf axils. Found on roadsides and in abandoned fields.

| 20-150cm ↑ |

MALVACEAE

1 2 3 4 5 6 7 8 9 10 11 12

Malva cretica Cav.
Malva cretica

This little mallow has hairy stems, erect or prostrate, and toothed leaves which vary in shape, the lower ones being almost rounded and the upper ones having very narrow lobes. The flowers have a diameter of up to 2cm and are light pink in colour with dark veining. A characteristic of the plant is the hypocalyx covered by the trilobate, pointed–tipped calyx that is twice its length. Found in barren, stony locations.

| 10-30cm ↑ |

MALVACEAE

1 2 3 4 5 6 7 8 9 10 11 12

Malva sylvestris L.
Common mallow

This is the most common of the mallows and the one which is mainly collected for pharmaceutical purposes. It is almost completely identical with *L. cretica* both in its leaves and flowers, but differs in the lobes of the calyx, which in this case are narrower. The plant can live for at least two years and is found in hedges, on roadsides, and in barren locations.

| 30-120cm ↑ |

MORACEAE

1 2 3 4 5 6 7 8 9 10 11 12

Ficus carica L.
Fig

This is one of the most common trees to be found in the Greek countryside; it grows very easily and is even found in the walls of ruined buildings. It has large palmately lobed leaves which, when cut, exude a milky liquid like the other parts of the plant. The flowers are tiny and hidden within the pear-shaped receptacle which, when ripe, constitutes one of the sweetest fruits – the fig.

| 2-5m ↑ |

Myrtus communis L.
Myrtle

1 2 3 4 5 6 7 8 9 10 11 12

The myrtle is a beautiful, evergreen bush which can reach a height of 3 metres and take a tree-like form. The leaves are opposite, elliptic, sharply pointed and very aromatic, since they have glands which produce essential oils. The flowers have 5 white petals, often with pink shading and typically with many stamens. The fruit is a berry, which becomes almost black during the ripening period.

| 1-4m ↑ |

Oxalis pes-caprae L.
Bermuda buttercup

1 2 3 4 5 6 7 8 9 10 11 12

This grassy weed with the brilliant yellow flowers which covers fields and olive groves from the beginning of spring onwards was only introduced to the Mediterranean area about 200 years ago. The leaves have a characteristic heart-shape which resemble a hoof (*pes-caprae* means goat's hoof) while the large, yellow flowers grow in umbels at the tips of the delicate stems. This is the most widely distributed of all the weeds and found normally in huge populations.

| 10-40cm ↑ |

● *Paeonia clusii* STERN & STEARN
Clusius's peony

1 2 3 4 5 6 7 8 9 10 11 12

One of the most beautiful peonies with brilliant white flowers, rarely pink, which can reach to a height of 12cm and have the scent of clove. The leaves are deeply cut, and smooth on both sides. Although it was discovered for the first time on Ida by Bellon, it is now only found in the White Mountains and on Dikti. In Sfakia it is called *Pseuthia* = 'the false one' because its flowers are so beautiful they almost look as if they are synthetic. In bygone days, Sfakian bridegrooms used to pin a peony in their lapels.

| 40-80cm ↑ |

| 1 | 2 | 3 | 4 | 5 | 6 | 7 | 8 | 9 | 10 | 11 | 12 |

Corydalis uniflora (Sieber) Nyman ●
Corydalis uniflora

This little plant which likes to hide among thorny bushes is endemic to Crete. It has slightly fleshy, opposite leaves. There is often only one flower, more rarely 2-3; the flower is white with pink blazons on the petals.
Found
in rocky
locations in the alpine
and sub-alpine zone.

| 10-15cm ↑ | 🏔 🦶

| 1 | 2 | 3 | 4 | 5 | 6 | 7 | 8 | 9 | 10 | 11 | 12 |

Fumaria capreolata L.
Ramping fumitory

The fumariae took their name from the aroma of smoke which they exude (*fumus* = smoke). *F. capreolata* has leaves divided into two or three segments, with sharply-pointed lobes.
The flowers are white or pink with very dark lips. The two sepals are ovate, slightly toothed and a little broader than the tube. Found in barren locations and in fields.

| 20-100cm ↑ | 🏔 🦶

| 1 | 2 | 3 | 4 | 5 | 6 | 7 | 8 | 9 | 10 | 11 | 12 |

Fumaria officinalis L.
Common fumitory

This is a branching plant with very dissected leaves that have narrow lobes. The flowers are whitish-pink with dark lips and the upper petal ends in a long spur, as is the case in all the fumariae. The sepals are lanceolate, and narrower than the tube. Found in stony places.

| 20-100cm ↑ | 🏔 🦶 🧍

Glaucium flavum Grantz
Yellow horned poppy

| 1 | 2 | 3 | 4 | 5 | 6 | 7 | 8 | 9 | 10 | 11 | 12 |

A small, biennial shrub with fleshy, grey-coloured, palmately lobed leaves, the lower ones very large with a short stalk, the upper ones stalkless. It has impressive, gold-yellow flowers with 4 overlapping petals. The fruit is a slender, cylindrical capsule which can exceed 20cm in length. Found on roadsides, on slopes, on sandy beaches, and amidst rubble.

 | 30-80cm ↑ |

Papaver argemone ssp. *nigrotinctum* (Fedde) Kadereit
Papaver argemone ssp. nigrotinctum

| 1 | 2 | 3 | 4 | 5 | 6 | 7 | 8 | 9 | 10 | 11 | 12 |

This variety, found in Greece, is a subspecies which was once considered a separate species in itself. The leaves are deeply divided with elongated lobes, and lanceolate. The stems are slightly hairy. The plant has a small red or orange flower, dark at the centre. The capsule is elongated and hairy.

P. apulum is similar, but differs in the shape of the capsule - in this case that of an egg; it is also very bristly.

 | 10-40cm ↑ |

Papaver purpureomarginatum Kadereit
Papaver purpureomarginatum

| 1 | 2 | 3 | 4 | 5 | 6 | 7 | 8 | 9 | 10 | 11 | 12 |

This plant has winged-lobed leaves, the lobes toothed and lanceolate. The stems are slender and slightly hairy. The flower is relatively small, not larger than 4cm. The petals are light-coloured, tending towards orange, without black at the base. The capsule is smooth, small, and elongated, and the anthers are yellow.

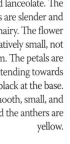

 | 10-40cm ↑ |

PAPAVERACEAE

| 1 | 2 | 3 | 4 | 5 | 6 | 7 | 8 | 9 | 10 | 11 | 12 |

Papaver rhoeas L.
Common poppy, corn poppy

The most common poppy. The leaves are deeply divided and toothed. The flower-stalks are very bristly. The petals are large (2-3cm), brilliant red, and often with a black fleck at the base. The capsules are short, almost spherical, smooth, and surrounded by many stamens with black or brown anthers. Found in cultivated and fallow fields, olive groves etc. Very widely distributed.

| 20-60cm ↑ |

PHYTOLACCACEAE

| 1 | 2 | 3 | 4 | 5 | 6 | 7 | 8 | 9 | 10 | 11 | 12 |

Phytolacca americana L.
American pokeweed

This plant originates from North America; it is self-sowing throughout Greece in fields, gardens and on roadsides. It has stems that are normally russet-coloured and large, lanceolate leaves which can reach a length of 30cm. The little white or pink flowers have only 5 sepals and grow in long racemes on stalks, opposite to the leaves. On ripening, the plant produces a fruit - a black berry - in very impressive bunches.

| 1-3m ↑ |

PLATANACEAE

| 1 | 2 | 3 | 4 | 5 | 6 | 7 | 8 | 9 | 10 | 11 | 12 |

Platanus orientalis L.
Oriental plane

This majestic, deciduous tree is well-loved in Greece and very often huge, ancient plane trees are to be found in village squares. It has large, palmately lobed leaves which are often toothed. The tree is connected with the kidnapping of Europa by the god Zeus, who had changed into a bull. The myth relates that the god took the beautiful young girl to Gortys and lay there with her under a plane tree which. Notwithstanding the myth, the plane tree at Gortys is of a particular evergreen, Cretan variety which is found sporadically all over the island.

| 3-20m ↑ |

Acantholimon androsaceum Boiss. / syn. *A. ulicinum, A. echinus* PLUMBAGINACEAE
Acantholimon androsaceum

`1 2 3 4 5 6 7 8 9 10 11 12`

A perennial phrygano plant which forms hemispherical bushes in the sub-alpine and alpine zone. It has dense foliage, with linear leaves that are sharply pointed and give the plant a spiky appearance. The flowers are pink with five petals which, when they fall, reveal membranous calyces with dark red stripes; thus even when all the flowers have finished, the plant still has a beautiful appearance. It prefers open, rocky, limestone locations.

| 10-50cm ↑ → | ▲ ▬

• *Limonium creticum* Artelari
Limonium creticum

PLUMBAGINACEAE

`1 2 3 4 5 6 7 8 9 10 11 12`

The limonia usually have slender, tough branching stems and leaves concentrated at the base. Their flowers have a characteristic membranous calyx. They prefer coastal locations and many of them are endemic with a narrow distribution, such as *L. creticum* which is found in front of the caves at Matala and is classified as vulnerable.

| 20-40cm ↑ | ▲ ⚓ ◈

Limonium sinuatum (L.) Mill.
Winged sea lavender

PLUMBAGINACEAE

`1 2 3 4 5 6 7 8 9 10 11 12`

L. sinuatum is a perennial with a wide distribution. It has winged leaves arranged in a rosette. The white flowers grow in dense corymbs and have a characteristic blue-violet, papery calyx. Also characteristic is the linear wing along the length of the stems.

| 20-40cm ↑ → | ▲ ⚓

POLYGALACEAE

1	2	3	4	5	6	7	8	9	10	11	12

Polygala venulosa Sm.
Milkwort

An herbaceous plant, with a much-branched stem and lanceolate, sharply-pointed leaves. The strange, zygomorphic, light blue flower consists of 5 unequal petals, 2 of which are atrophied, the lower one torn into a fringe. Likewise, of the 5 sepals two are very large and butterfly-shaped, with characteristic veining. It is believed that animals which graze on this plant produce more milk, a characteristic which has given the genus its name (*polygala* = much milk). Found in stony places, often amongst phrygana and bushes.

 | 30cm ↑→ |

POLYGONACEAE

1	2	3	4	5	6	7	8	9	10	11	12

Polygonum idaeum Hayek ●
Polygonum idaeum

This dwarf plant with the small ovate leaves which conceal a huge woody root is endemic to Crete, and covers the Nida High Plateau like grass. It imparts a gold colour to the teeth of animals that eat it, a fact which in times past led to the fabrication of a myth that there was gold to be found on Psiloritis.

 | 1-3cm ↑ |

PORTULACACEAE

1	2	3	4	5	6	7	8	9	10	11	12

Portulaca oleracea L.
Purslane

An herbaceous plant, rather creeping, with branching stems and leaves that are inverse-ovate, fleshy and smooth, often with dark shading on the lips. The flowers are yellow and grow in the leaf axils or at the ends of the stems in small groups. It is used in salads and is commonly found in gardens and fields.

 | 20-50cm ↑→ |

Anagallis arvensis L.
Pimpernel

A small herbaceous plant, erect or prostrate with ovate-lanceolate, opposite leaves, stalkless and smooth. The orange-red or blue flowers grow on slender flower-stalks in the leaf axils. The edges of the petals bear little hairs which differentiate this species from the very similar *A. foemina*. Found in cultivated and fallow fields, ditches, and phrygana.

| 10-40cm ↑ → |

Cyclamen creticum (Doerfl) Hildebr.
Cretan sowbread

The endemic Cretan cyclamen is pure white but can often be found with slight pink shading. It has a corolla without protuberances and leaves which resemble those of the ivy. Found in damp, shaded locations.

| 5-15cm ↑ |

Cyclamen graecum Link
Greek sowbread

This has heart-shaped leaves with light-coloured markings, and red shading on the underside. The flowers are whitish-pink with dark pink lines and corollary protuberances; they appear in autumn. Found in stony locations.

| 5-15cm ↑ |

Cyclamen hederifolium Aiton / syn. *C. neopolitanum*
Ivy-leaved Sowbread

| 1 | 2 | 3 | 4 | 5 | 6 | 7 | 8 | 9 | 10 | 11 | 12 |

This plant has leaves resembling those of the ivy (*hedera*) – hence the name. It has a very large, flattish tuber. The flowers are light pink with dark corollary protuberances. It flowers in the autumn in cool, shady locations, and is commonly cultivated.

| 5-10cm ↑ |

Lysimachia serpyllifolia Schreb. ●
Lysimachia serpyllifolia

| 1 | 2 | 3 | 4 | 5 | 6 | 7 | 8 | 9 | 10 | 11 | 12 |

This little endemic plant has many stems and opposite leaves which are ovate and sharply pointed. The little yellow flowers have a diameter of 1–1.5cm, and are solitary, growing from the leaf axils. The fruits are small, spherical capsules which resemble the marbles that children use to play a game. The plant, which bears the name of the ancient physician Lysimachus of Kos, is found in stony locations in the mountain and alpine zone, often amongst other plants.

| 5-15cm ↑ → |

Primula vulgaris Huds.
Primrose

| 1 | 2 | 3 | 4 | 5 | 6 | 7 | 8 | 9 | 10 | 11 | 12 |

The common primula is a very beautiful plant, almost without a stem and with inverse-ovate leaves that are corrugated, up to 15cm long, and very narrow at the base. The fragrant, whitish-yellow flowers are solitary, on a long flower-stalk, and have a diameter of up to 4cm. The downy calyx has 5 lanceolate, sharply-pointed lobes and reaches half-way up the tube. A very decorative plant, found in fields, meadows, clearings and damp locations.

| 10-30cm ↑ |

Punica granatum L.
Pomegranate

PUNICACEAE

| 1 | 2 | 3 | 4 | 5 | 6 | 7 | 8 | 9 | 10 | 11 | 12 |

The pomegranate, mentioned in Homer, is a spiny tree with ovate, opposite, and leathery leaves. It produces beautiful, large very red flowers which form a round red fruit with a diameter that can be as much as 10cm – the pomegranate – containing hundreds of sweet, deep-red seeds. The skin of the pomegranate fruit is used as a natural dye and produces wonderful yellow-brown, earthy colours. Found in gardens, on the edges of fields, and in coppices.

| 2-7m ↑ |

Cytinus hypocistis L.
Cytinus

RAFFLESIACEAE

| 1 | 2 | 3 | 4 | 5 | 6 | 7 | 8 | 9 | 10 | 11 | 12 |

This peculiar, chlorophyll-free plant with its blindingly red colour grows as a parasite on the roots of ladania. It has red fleshy leaves that cover each other in succession. The flower has 4 petals, white or yellow, covered by the leaves, in dense heads, the outer flowers being male, the inner ones female. The name *hypocistis* originates from Dioscurides. Cytinus belongs to the same family as *Raflesia*, a tropical plant whose flower is the largest in the world with a diameter of 1 metre.

| 5-10cm ↑ |

Adonis microcarpa DC.
Yellow pheasant's eye

RANUNCULACEAE

| 1 | 2 | 3 | 4 | 5 | 6 | 7 | 8 | 9 | 10 | 11 | 12 |

An annual herbaceous plant with wing-shaped leaves, torn and thread-like. The flowers are yellow, with five sepals and 6-10 petals. Found in stony locations and fields.

| 10-40cm ↑ |

RANUNCULACEAE

| 1 | 2 | 3 | 4 | 5 | 6 | 7 | 8 | 9 | 10 | 11 | 12 |

Anemone coronaria L.
Crown or poppy anemone

The leaves of the whorl and base are deeply cut. The flowers are large, usually with five sepals, sometimes many more, with a length of up to 4cm and a number of blackish-mauve anthers. The colours of the sepals are numerous, most commonly red, white, violet, blue and pink. Their shape also varies, from round to pointed-tipped. The result is a multitude of varieties which often form a really polychrome carpet in olive groves and fields.

 | 20-30cm ↑ |

RANUNCULACEAE   ## *Anemone hortensis* **ssp.** *heldreichii* (Boiss.) Rech. ●

| 1 | 2 | 3 | 4 | 5 | 6 | 7 | 8 | 9 | 10 | 11 | 12 |

Anemone hortensis

This plant is endemic to Crete and Karpathos. The leaves of the whorl are entire or trilobate, lanceolate, and the lower ones are deeply palmately lobed with strongly toothed lobes. The flower has many sepals, more than 10, which are white or pink and often blue at the base; the anthers are violet. Found in phrygana, olive groves, and stony places.

 | 15-45cm ↑

RANUNCULACEAE

| 1 | 2 | 3 | 4 | 5 | 6 | 7 | 8 | 9 | 10 | 11 | 12 |

Clematis cirrhosa L.
Virgin's bower

An evergreen, climbing bush with woody stems and smooth, saw-edged leaves. The five-part, bell-shaped whitish-yellow flowers grow on the stems from the previous year. This wild vine flowers in autumn and winter and often the flowers are so numerous that they cover the plant. On maturity, a multitude of fine hairs create the impression of a white comet. Found in hedgerows and in the zone of Mediterranean maquis.

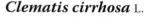 | 1-3m ↑→ |

Delphinium staphisagria L.
Delphinium

RANUNCULACEAE

| 1 | 2 | 3 | 4 | 5 | 6 | 7 | 8 | 9 | 10 | 11 | 12 |

A hairy plant with a strong stem and height which often exceeds 1 metre. It has large, palmately lobed leaves, the lobes themselves either entire or trilobate, and sharply pointed. The azure or darker blue zygomorphic flowers are in a raceme at the end of the stem and distinguished by their characteristic, very short spur. The dust from the seeds has been used since antiquity to kill lice. Found in barren, stony places, fields and on roadsides.

| 50-100m ↑ | ⛰ 🌱 🏺 ☠

Nigella damascena L.
Love-in-a-mist, or Devil-in-a-bush

RANUNCULACEAE

| 1 | 2 | 3 | 4 | 5 | 6 | 7 | 8 | 9 | 10 | 11 | 12 |

This herbaceous plant with the unusual flower has a slender, erect, and angular stem and very dissected leaves with thread-like lobes. The bracts of the flowers resemble the leaves – this is typical of the plant. The flower has 5 bluish-white sepals, many stamens and an ovary consisting partly of pockets with characteristically short 'beaks', which on maturity form a very swollen capsule. Found in fields, phrygana, olive groves, and on roadsides. It is cultivated as a decorative plant.

| 10-50cm ↑ | ⛰ 🌱 🪴

Ranunculus asiaticus L.
Turban buttercup

RANUNCULACEAE

| 1 | 2 | 3 | 4 | 5 | 6 | 7 | 8 | 9 | 10 | 11 | 12 |

R. asiaticus, a plant from the eastern Mediterranean, is one of the most beautiful of the ranunculi. It is a perennial with an erect, hairy stem; the leaves at the base are ovate and toothed, in contrast to the upper leaves which are deeply dissected. The flower is usually white or pink, more rarely red or yellow with 5 or more petals and 5 narrow ovate greenish sepals, a characteristic generally differentiating the ranunculi from the anemones with which they are often confused.

| 15-30cm ↑ | ⛰ 🌱 ☠

RANUNCULACEAE

| 1 | 2 | 3 | 4 | 5 | 6 | 7 | 8 | 9 | 10 | 11 | 12 |

Ranunculus bullatus L.
Ranunculus bullatus

One of the few ranunculi which flower in the autumn. It has a hairy, erect stem and ovate leaves, delicately toothed and stalked, which are all concentrated in a rosette at the base of the plant. The flowers are yellow with 5-12 petals and many stamens. Found in phrygana, stony locations, and on slopes.

| 10-20cm ↑ |

RANUNCULACEAE

| 1 | 2 | 3 | 4 | 5 | 6 | 7 | 8 | 9 | 10 | 11 | 12 |

Ranunculus creticus L.
Ranunculus creticus

A perennial with an erect, hairy and branching stem. The leaves are large, up to 12cm, and kidney-shaped with toothed lobes. The flowers are yellow with a diameter of up to 3cm. Endemic to the south-east Aegean, it prefers shady slopes, ditches, and damp places.

| 20-50cm ↑ |

RANUNCULACEAE

| 1 | 2 | 3 | 4 | 5 | 6 | 7 | 8 | 9 | 10 | 11 | 12 |

Ranunculus cupreus BOISS. & HELDR. ●
Ranunculus cupreus

A perennial with an erect, downy stem and basal leaves with two winged lobes, the latter being broad. Usually 1 flower, which is yellow. The lower part of the petals is decorated with beautiful, copper-coloured stipples, a characteristic which gives the plant its name. It is endemic to Crete and found in stony places, on slopes and in phrygana.

| 10-20cm ↑ |

Ranunculus ficaria L.
Lesser celandine

| 1 | 2 | 3 | 4 | 5 | 6 | 7 | 8 | 9 | 10 | 11 | 12 |

A perennial plant with many forms. The stem is smooth and the leaves are deep green, smooth, and heart-shaped with a long stalk. The flowers are solitary, as is the case with nearly all the ranunculi; they are yellow with 8-12 narrow, glossy petals and 3 sepals which are half the length of the petals. Found in damp, shady locations.

| 5-30cm ↑

Reseda alba L.
White mignonette

| 1 | 2 | 3 | 4 | 5 | 6 | 7 | 8 | 9 | 10 | 11 | 12 |

The white reseda has an erect stem with alternate leaves, deeply divided and with lanceolate, wavy lobes. The small, white flowers are arranged in a dense ear-like inflorescence and have 5 fringed petals and 5 smaller sepals. Found in barren, stony locations, on sandy beaches and in fields. The name of the genus comes from the Latin *resido*, meaning relax and refers to the supposed soothing properties of the plant.

| 30-80cm ↑

Reseda lutea L.
Wild mignonette

| 1 | 2 | 3 | 4 | 5 | 6 | 7 | 8 | 9 | 10 | 11 | 12 |

The yellow reseda is a slightly smaller plant with undulating leaves, very dissected and with narrow lobes. Its flowers are arranged in a spike similar to that of *R. alba*, but the florets are ochre-yellow with 6 petals and the same number of sepals. Found in barren places, fields, and on roadsides.

| 20-60cm ↑

RESEDACEAE

| 1 | 2 | 3 | 4 | 5 | 6 | 7 | 8 | 9 | 10 | 11 | 12 |

Reseda luteola L.
Weld, Dyer's rocket

This has lanceolate, entire leaves, and flowers with 4 sepals and the same number of fringed petals. The leaves of the plant contain very strong pigments, which were known to Dioscurides. The colours they produce range from yellow to an oil shade, and there are Coptic fabrics more than 1,500 years old which were dyed with them and still retain their colour. Found in barren places, on roadsides, on slopes, and in ruins.

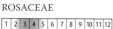 | 20-60cm ↑ |

ROSACEAE **Amelanchier ovalis ssp. cretica** (WILLD) MAIRE & PETITM. ●
Amelanchier ovalis ssp. cretica

A shrub or tree with branching stems and ovate leaves which are downy in the young plant and become smooth later on. The shape of the leaves gives the name to the species. The flowers are white and grow in terminal racemes. The plant is found sporadically in the White Mountains and on Psiloritis.

| 2-3m ↑ |

ROSACEAE

| 1 | 2 | 3 | 4 | 5 | 6 | 7 | 8 | 9 | 10 | 11 | 12 |

Crataegus monogyna Jacq.
Hawthorn

A spiny, much-branching shrub or tree with three or five-lobed leaves. The flowers are white with five petals, and the fruits are small red berries. On Crete, the subspecies *azarella* is found on the edges of fields, on slopes, in thickets and forests.

| 2-5m ↑ |

Prunus prostrata LEBILL.
Prostrate cherry

ROSACEAE

| 1 | 2 | 3 | 4 | 5 | 6 | 7 | 8 | 9 | 10 | 11 | 12 |

A small, deciduous creeping shrub which likes to hug rocks and stones, presenting a unique picture during the flowering period. It has crooked, woody stems and small leaves that are ovate or elliptic and saw-edged. The flowers are whitish-pink in colour and the fruits are small, red berries. Found on rocks in the mountain and alpine zone.

| 0,30-2m →

Prunus webbii (SPACH) VIERH. / syn. *Amygdalus webbii*
Prunus webbii

ROSACEAE

| 1 | 2 | 3 | 4 | 5 | 6 | 7 | 8 | 9 | 10 | 11 | 12 |

The bitter almond is a much-branching shrub with spiny stems and small, ovate-elongated leaves. The flowers are white or rose-coloured with a diameter which does not exceed 2.5cm.
It flowers at the end of winter and is found in olive groves, rocky places and on the edges of fields.

| 1-3m ↑ |

Rosa canina L. / syn. *Rosa corymbifera*
Dog rose

ROSACEAE

| 1 | 2 | 3 | 4 | 5 | 6 | 7 | 8 | 9 | 10 | 11 | 12 |

A bush with very thorny branches and a height of up to 3 metres. The thorns are curved with a flat base. The flowers are pink, rarely white, solitary or more usually in corymbs of 3-10 with a diameter of up to 6cm. The leaves have 5-7 leaflets, 3-5cm, and are ovate, smooth, and lanceolate at the tips, saw-edged with relatively large teeth. The fruit is ovoid, and red. Found in thickets and in rocky places.

| 1-3m ↑ |

ROSACEAE

1 2 3 **4 5 6 7** 8 9 10 11 12

Rosa pulverulenta M. Bieb. / syn. *Rosa glutinosa*

Rosa pulverulenta

A small bush with strong stems and thorns that are light in colour, linear or slightly curved. The leaves have 5-7 leaflets and are almost round, toothed and with many glands which give them a dusty texture. The flowers are solitary, and are white or light pink in colour on short flower-stalks. Found in the mountain zone throughout almost the whole of Greece.

| 1-1,50m ↑ |

ROSACEAE

1 2 3 **4 5 6 7** 8 9 10 11 12

Rosa sempervirens L.

Rosa sempervirens

A perennial shrub, the only ever-green of all the wild roses, with many long, climbing branches which reach to a great height. The leaves have 3-7 leaflets which are lanceolate, saw-edged, and smooth with a leathery texture. The flowers are white and arranged in corymbs of 3-10, with 5 petals and a diameter of up to 6cm. Blooming is so profuse that the flower-bearing stems almost disappear beneath the multitude of flowers. Found in forested areas and thickets.

| 2-8m ↑ |

ROSACEAE

1 2 3 4 5 **6 7 8 9** 10 11 12

Rubus sanctus Schreb. / syn. *Rubus ulmifolius*

Bramble, blackberry

This is the burning bush of the Bible, hence its name. It is a perennial, climbing and branching bush with long, slender stems that are very thorny. The leaves are composite with 3-5 ovate, toothed leaflets, lighter coloured on the underside. The flowers are about 2cm in diameter with long thorny stalks, arranged in loose spikes. There are 5 petals, white or pink, and numerous stamens. The fruits – blackberries – are edible. Normally found on the edges of fields, in hedgerows, and abandoned fields.

| 1-2m ↑→ |

Sarcopoterium spinosum (L.) SPACH

Thorny burnet

ROSACEAE

| 1 | 2 | 3 | 4 | 5 | 6 | 7 | 8 | 9 | 10 | 11 | 12 |

A perennial, dense, head-shaped phrygano plant, very thorny, and similar in form to *E. akantothmnos*. The leaves are small and consist of many leaflets. The beautiful, small, red fleshy fruits are very characteristic. Found in phrygana and in thickets.

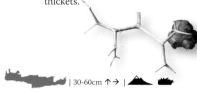

| 30-60cm ↑ →

● *Asperula idaea* HALÁCSY

Asperula idaea

RUBIACEAE

| 1 | 2 | 3 | 4 | 5 | 6 | 7 | 8 | 9 | 10 | 11 | 12 |

The asperulas are little herbaceous or phrygano plants which have typically small flowers with a long tube, often pink or white, and quadrangular stems. *A. idaea* is a small, perennial, much-branching phrygano with small, sharply-pointed linear leaves. The flowers are pink, very slightly downy and in clusters. Found in stony locations in the three great mountain massifs of Crete.

| 10-20cm ↑ |

● *Asperula incana* SM. / syn. *Asperula pubescens*

Asperula incana

RUBIACEAE

| 1 | 2 | 3 | 4 | 5 | 6 | 7 | 8 | 9 | 10 | 11 | 12 |

A. incana is a perennial, small and hairy phrygano plant with linear leaves, sharply pointed at the tip, which grow in whorls of 6. The flowers are pink with a long tube, in dense heads. Found in rocky locations, phrygana, and on slopes.

| 20-40cm ↑ |

RUBIACEAE

| 1 | 2 | 3 | 4 | 5 | 6 | 7 | 8 | 9 | 10 | 11 | 12 |

Asperula rigida M. ●
Asperula rigida

A small, branching shrub or phrygano plant with woody stems and drooping linear leaves that are smooth and arranged in whorls. The inflorescences have a few (1-5) flowers, which are white or pink in terminal clusters. Endemic to Crete, and found on rocky cliffs, slopes and in stony locations.

 | 20-40cm ↑ |

RUBIACEAE

| 1 | 2 | 3 | 4 | 5 | 6 | 7 | 8 | 9 | 10 | 11 | 12 |

Putoria calabrica (L.F.) DC.
Putoria

A small, normally spreading, phrygana plant with a rank odour. It has a woody stem and opposite leaves which are lanceolate, fleshy and smooth. The flowers resemble those of asperula, and have 4 triangular lobes, a long tube, and develop in corymbs. Found in rocky places from the coastal to the alpine zone.

 | 10-25cm → |

RUTACEAE

| 1 | 2 | 3 | 4 | 5 | 6 | 7 | 8 | 9 | 10 | 11 | 12 |

Ruta chalepensis L.
Fringed rue

A perennial, herbaceous plant or small shrub with erect stems, becoming woody at the base, and deeply-cut leaves with ovate, elongated lobes. The yellow flowers have 4-5 ovate, very characteristic fringed petals and flat lanceolate, stippled sepals. The plant, which emits a heavy scent, has been used from the past to this day as a menstrual stimulant. Found in rocky places, amidst ruins, and in gorges.

| 20-80cm → |

Saxifraga chrysosplenifolia Boiss.

Saxifraga chrysosplenifolia

SAXIFRAGACEAE

1 2 3 4 5 6 7 8 9 10 11 12

A perennial, herbaceous plant with kidney-shaped leaves, toothed, rather fleshy and stalked; the leaves on the stem are stalkless. The flowers have ovate petals which are white with red spots. The name of the genus comes from the Latin, meaning 'that which breaks the rocks', probably referring to the picture presented by the plant which usually grows amongst clefts in rocks. The plant is endemic to the southern Balkans.

| 10-50cm →

Bellardia trixago (L.) All.

Bellardia

SCROPHULARIACEAE

1 2 3 4 5 6 7 8 9 10 11 12

This is an elegant, perennial herbaceous plant with a strong, erect stem and opposite leaves which are downy, elongated, toothed, usually fleshy, and often have a russet-coloured lip. The whitish-pink flowers are arranged in typical pyramid-shaped spikes. Every flower has a large, undivided lower lip, the upper lip smaller and trilobate, and grows from the four-lobed downy calyx. Found in phrygana and fields.

| 10-50cm ↑

Parentucellia latifolia (L.) Caruel

Southern red bartsia

SCROPHULARIACEAE

1 2 3 4 5 6 7 8 9 10 11 12

This small, hairy, herbaceous annual has an erect stem, often russet-coloured, and small, deeply toothed and opposite leaves. The tiny, reddish-pink flowers have a trilobate lower lip, a tubular toothed calyx, and develop in the form of a dense ear. It is a semi-parasitic plant which absorbs nutrients from the rhizomes of plants in its neighbourhood. Found in stony locations, phrygana, and on the perimeters of fields.

| 5-25cm ↑

SCROPHULARIACEAE

`1` `2` `3` `4` `5` `6` `7` `8` `9` `10` `11` `12`

Parentucellia viscosa (L.) Caruel
Yellow bartsia

A glandy, hairy herbaceous plant with an erect stem. The leaves and bracts are opposite, lanceolate, and saw-edged. The flowers are arranged in a terminal, elongated spike, yellow, with a large, trilobate lower lip and a tubular calyx with long lobes. Found in damp places, on the banks of streams, and in fields.

| 10-50cm ↑ |

SCROPHULARIACEAE

`1` `2` `3` `4` `5` `6` `7` `8` `9` `10` `11` `12`

Scrophularia heterophylla Willd.
Scrophularia heterophylla

The scrophulariae are herbaceous plants, usually strong-smelling, with small, almost round and bag-like flowers which are partly covered by little sepals. *S. heterophylla* has deeply-toothed leaves, toothed or deeply torn and rather fleshy. The flowers are dark red with a white lip in a loose, pyramid-shaped and leafless spike. Found amidst old walls and on rocky slopes, often near the sea.

| 30-80cm ↑ |

SCROPHULARIACEAE

`1` `2` `3` `4` `5` `6` `7` `8` `9` `10` `11` `12`

Scrophularia lucida L.
Scrophularia lucida

A perennial, hairless plant with a strong stem, russet-coloured and branching, and opposite leaves, deeply divided with narrow, toothed lobes. The flowers are greenish-red and arranged in elongated, leafless, pyramid-shaped spikes. The two butterfly-shaped petals and semi-circular sepals which have white, membranous lips are characteristic. Found in fields, on roadsides, and on slopes.

| 30-80cm ↑ |

Scrophularia peregrina L.
Nettle-leaved figwort

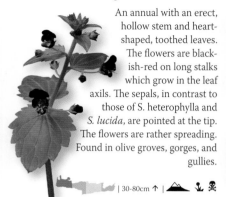

An annual with an erect, hollow stem and heart-shaped, toothed leaves. The flowers are blackish-red on long stalks which grow in the leaf axils. The sepals, in contrast to those of S. heterophylla and *S. lucida*, are pointed at the tip. The flowers are rather spreading. Found in olive groves, gorges, and gullies.

| 30-80cm ↑ |

● *Verbascum arcturus* L.
Verbascum arcturus

The mulleins, as the various species of *Verbascum* are generally known, are downy, herbaceous or phrygano plants with flowers consisting of five parts and usually yellow. More than 40 species grow in Greece; some of these are endemic, such as *V. arcturus* which is only found on Crete. It has an erect stem and toothed, very hairy leaves concentrated at the base. The flowers are yellow with a long stalk, in loose, elongated and pyramid-shaped spikes. Found on vertical cliffs and slopes, and often in ravines.

| 30-70cm ↑ |

Verbascum macrurum TEN.
Verbascum macrurum

A biennial, downy plant which reaches an impressive height. It has large, stalkless, rather wavy lanceolate leaves with strong veining. The flowers are stalkless and arranged in a very dense, intensely hairy, ear-like inflorescence. Found in stony places, barren fields and on roadsides.

| 0,50-1.50m ↑ |

SCROPHULARIACEAE

| 1 | 2 | 3 | 4 | 5 | 6 | 7 | 8 | 9 | 10 | 11 | 12 |

Verbascum sinuatum L.

Verbascum sinuatum

This is the most frequently occurring species of *Verbascum*; the leaves at the base are large and deeply divided with a very undulating lip. A number of smaller stems grow out from the central stem and all bear many little axillary groups of a few flowers along their length. Found in fields, sandy locations, and on roadsides.

| 0.50-1.50m ↑ |

SCROPHULARIACEAE

| 1 | 2 | 3 | 4 | 5 | 6 | 7 | 8 | 9 | 10 | 11 | 12 |

Verbascum spinosum L. ●

Spiny mullein

A beautiful perennial phrygano plant which forms hemispherical clumps. The stems are branching, very spiny and have small, lanceolate, downy leaves. The flowers are yellow, solitary, and with a diameter of up to 2cm. Found in stony locations in the White Mountains.

| 20-50cm ↑ → |

SCROPHULARIACEAE

| 1 | 2 | 3 | 4 | 5 | 6 | 7 | 8 | 9 | 10 | 11 | 12 |

Veronica thymifolia Sm. ●

Veronica thymifolia

This little veronica is endemic to Greece and grows in stony places at alpine altitudes. It is a downy plant with a woody stem and elongated leaves whose lips are turned downwards. The flowers are pink or blue with a four-lobed calyx. Found on the great mountains of Crete.

| 5-15cm ↑ → |

Datura stramonium L.
Thorn apple

1	2	3	4	5	6	7	8	9	10	11	12

This is a rank-smelling, poisonous and hallucinogenic plant, due to the active constituents it contains - hyoscyamine, scopolamine and atropine. The plant is of American origin; it is an annual and has large, usually palmately lobed leaves. The flowers are white, trumpet-like and can reach a length of 10cm. Found on waste ground, amidst rubble, on roadsides and in ditches.

| 0.40-1.20m ↑ |

Hyoscyamus albus L.
White henbane

1	2	3	4	5	6	7	8	9	10	11	12

This is also a poisonous plant which is avoided by all animals except for the pig – hence the name *Hyoscyamus* which means 'pig-bean' and derives from the Greek words *hys* (pig) and *kyamos* (bean). The large, hairy, soft leaves are toothed; more rarely they are almost entire. It has yellowish tubular flowers with unequal lips and a large, hairy calyx with triangular lobes. Found in wasteland, amidst rubble, and on roadsides.

| 30-90cm ↑ → |

Mandragora autumnalis BERTOL. / syn. *Mandragora officinarum*   SOLANACEAE
Mandrake

1	2	3	4	5	6	7	8	9	10	11	12

The anthropomorphic root of the mandrake, combined with its medicinal properties which have been known since antiquity, is the reason why there are so many beliefs about the plant. The very large leaves grow almost immediately from the roots and form an impressive prostrate rosette, in the centre of which the blue-violet bell-shaped flowers develop. Found in stony locations and barren fields.

| 20-50cm ↑ → |

SOLANACEAE

| 1 | 2 | 3 | 4 | 5 | 6 | 7 | 8 | 9 | 10 | 11 | 12 |

Nicotiana glauca GRAHAM
Tree tobacco

This is a naturalised tree or bush which originated from South America. The flowers are tubular and yellow, with a diameter of about 5mm and a length of 3-4cm, and arranged in loose spikes. The leaves are lanceolate and grey - hence the name. It is cultivated as a decorative plant and is self-sowing on old walls, cliffs, roadsides and in abandoned fields. It flowers nearly the whole year round. Many parts of the plant are poisonous.

| 2-5m ↑ |

STYRACACEAE

| 1 | 2 | 3 | 4 | 5 | 6 | 7 | 8 | 9 | 10 | 11 | 12 |

Styrax officinalis L.
Storax

A small tree or bush with ovate, slightly downy leaves. The white, bell-like and nodding flowers are very fragrant and grow in bunches. According to the myth, the plant originated from Crete and was introduced to mainland Greece by Radamanthys, the brother of Minos; both were sons of Zeus and Europa. Found in cool locations, on the banks of rivers and in the zone of Mediterranean maquis.

| 2-5m ↑ |

THYMELAEACEAE

| 1 | 2 | 3 | 4 | 5 | 6 | 7 | 8 | 9 | 10 | 11 | 12 |

Daphne gnidioides JAUB. & SPACH
Daphne gnidioides

Daphne gnidioides is a dense shrub with inverse-lanceolate (oblong-lanceolate), fleshy leaves. The flowers are whitish-yellow and appear along with the red fruits. Found in stony places near the sea.

| 0,5-2m ↑ |

Daphne oleoides Schreb.
Daphne oleoides

| 1 | 2 | 3 | 4 | 5 | 6 | 7 | 8 | 9 | 10 | 11 | 12 |

The scientific name of these shrubs - *Daphne* - causes confusion in Greece since, from ancient times, the name *daphni* has been given to that other plant unfortunately baptized *Laurus nobilis* (bay) by Linnaeus. *D. oleoides* is a shrub with fleshy, ovate leaves and beautiful white, fragrant flowers with 4 long, pointed-tipped lobes which grow in groups of 3-6 in terminal, head-like bunches. Found in alpine, mountainous and rocky locations, in thickets and in open forests.

| 20-80cm ↑

Daphne sericea Vahl.
Daphne sericea

| 1 | 2 | 3 | 4 | 5 | 6 | 7 | 8 | 9 | 10 | 11 | 12 |

This beautiful, much-branched shrub has leaves that are hairy on the underside, lanceolate, and rather fleshy. The fragrant flowers, which have a silky texture, are hairy on the outside and grow in bunches. They are usually pink, but on maturity acquire shades of cream. Found in stony locations, usually in the mountain zone.

| 20-60cm ↑

Thymelaea hirsuta (L.) Endl.
Thymelaea hirsuta

| 1 | 2 | 3 | 4 | 5 | 6 | 7 | 8 | 9 | 10 | 11 | 12 |

A much-branched shrub with densely downy stems. The leaves are numerous, small, fleshy and overlapping. The yellow flowers grow in bunches and appear in autumn; flowering often continues until the spring. Found in stony locations, near the sea.

| 40-100cm ↑

THYMELEACEAE

| 1 | 2 | 3 | 4 | 5 | 6 | 7 | 8 | 9 | 10 | 11 | 12 |

Thymelaea tartonraira (L.) ALL.
Thymelaea tartonraira

A small, much-branched phrygano plant or shrub with lanceolate, silver-coloured and hairy leaves. The flowers are axillary, yellow with 4 sharply-pointed lobes and downy on the outside, often many together. Found in stony locations, phrygana, and on slopes.

| 20-50cm ↑ |

ULMACEAE

| 1 | 2 | 3 | 4 | 5 | 6 | 7 | 8 | 9 | 10 | 11 | 12 |

Zelkova abelicea (LAM.) BOISS. / syn. *Zelkova cretica* ●
Zelkova abelicea

Endemic to the mountains of Crete, Zelkova is the only representative of this Asiatic genus in Europe. It was from the branches of this rare tree that shepherds used to make their crooks, and since it bore no resemblance to any other tree in the Cretan mountains they called it *anégnoro*, meaning unrecognisable. The very tiny population of this unique tree, which has been characterized as threatened, is in need of protection.

| 2-10m ↑ |

UMBELLIFERAE

| 1 | 2 | 3 | 4 | 5 | 6 | 7 | 8 | 9 | 10 | 11 | 12 |

Bupleurum kakiscalae GREUTER ●
Bupleurum kakiscalae

This large-leaved umbellifer which forms impressive rosettes and whose biological cycle has not yet been exhaustively studied, flowers after the fourth year of its life. The little yellow flowers appear in an umbel. The plant is found in a single rocky location in the White Mountains and given the small number of examples in existence, it is easy to understand that it really does constitute an endangered species. The name kakiscalae derives from the locality where the plant is to be found.

| 0,5-1m ↑ |

Conium maculatum L.
Hemlock

This is the most famous of the umbelliferae, since it was the poison of this plant that killed Socrates, the greatest of the philosophers. The plant received its name in antiquity due to the funnel-like leaves which are deeply divided with toothed lobes. It has a much-branching habit with ridged, hollow stems.The umbel with the little white flowers has up to 20 rays that are uneven in length. Found on the edges of fields, in hedgerows, and amidst rubble.

| 50-100cm ↑ |

Daucus carota L.
Wild carrot

This is a polymorphic plant with a branching stem and deeply-divided leaves. The umbels are large with a multitude of rays and the flowers white or purple, always with dark purple at the centre. After flowering, the umbel closes to form a ball. The plant, which has a tuberous rhizome, is the progenitor of the cultivated carrot. Found in fields and on roadsides.

| 30-80cm ↑ |

Eryngium campestre L.
Field eryngo

A perennial plant, light green in colour with a tough, branching stem and leathery leaves with broad, spiny lobes. Small flowers in spherical heads which have large, elongated and spiny bracts. Found in meadows, phrygana, abandoned fields, and coastal places.

| 30-60cm ↑ |

| 1 | 2 | 3 | 4 | 5 | 6 | 7 | 8 | 9 | 10 | 11 | 12 |

Eryngium creticum Lam.
Small-headed blue eryngo

Despite its name (*creticum*) this plant has a distribution from the Balkans to the Middle East.
It is a perennial with branching stems and spiny leaves that are a variety of shapes. The flowers are in small round heads which have up to 7 elongated, spiny bracts. The whole plant is an impressive bluish-violet colour. Found on wasteland, in stony places, and in abandoned fields.

| 15-60cm ↑ |

| 1 | 2 | 3 | 4 | 5 | 6 | 7 | 8 | 9 | 10 | 11 | 12 |

Eryngium maritimum L.
Sea holly

This plant has characteristic large, spiny and palmately lobed periblastic leaves and branching stems which are grey or violet in colour.
The little, bluish-white flowers occur in round heads which have wide, spiny bracts. Found on sandy beaches.

| 15-60cm ↑ |

| 1 | 2 | 3 | 4 | 5 | 6 | 7 | 8 | 9 | 10 | 11 | 12 |

Ferula communis L.
Giant fennel

This is a perennial plant with a large, thick, light stem and deeply-cut leaves which re-semble those of fennel. The yellow flowers are arranged in terminal, round umbels which have up to 40 rays. In the past, the dried stems of the plant were used to make im-promptu furniture. The fleshy content of the stems burns slowly, and for this reason it was used to make torches in antiquity. It is with such a torch that, according to mythology, *Prometheus* brought fire to the human race. Found on roadsides, cliffs, and in fields.

| 1-2m ↑ |

Ferulago nodosa (L.) Boiss.
Ferulago

A  plant resembling *Ferula*, but differentiated from it by the presence of round swellings at the places where the stems branch, which give it its name (nodosa). The leaves are deeply cut with straight lobes and are all concentrated at the base of the plant. The yellow flowers are arranged in an umbel which has up to 15 rays. Found in stony places and barren fields.

| 0,5-2m ↑ |

Lecokia cretica (Lam.) DC.
Lecokia cretica

This is a plant from south-west Asia and in the whole of Europe is found only on Crete. It is a perennial with many, smooth leaves divided into three parts with toothed leaflets. The flowers are white or ochre-yellow in an umbel of 8-18 rays. The fruits are ovoid, roughly haired. Found in olive groves, shady, damp locations, and ditches.

| 40-80cm ↑ |

Oenanthe pimpinelloides L.
Tubular water dropwort

A plant with a hollow stem, characteristically fluted, and leaves divided into two wings with sphenoid lobes; the upper leaves have linear lobes. The flowers are white, in umbels with 5-15 rays resembling little stems. Found in ditches, damp locations, and on roadsides.

| 40-60cm ↑ |

UMBELLIFERAE

1 2 3 4 5 6 7 8 9 10 11 12

Opopanax hispidus Griseb
Opopanax hispidus

A relatively rare plant, hairy and branching. Large, deeply-divided leaves with ovate, toothed lobes. The flowers are yellow in umbels of up to 16 rays. The plant is medicinal and aromatic, and was probably the 'panacaea' of Theophrastus; at any rate, the name derives from the Greek words '*opós*' ('juice') and '*panákeia*' ('medicine for all ills'). The plant is found in scattered distribution throughout the island in dry locations, phrygana, and olive groves.

 | 0,5-2m ↑ |

UMBELLIFERAE

1 2 3 4 5 6 7 8 9 10 11 12

Orlaya grandiflora (L.) Hoffm.
Orlaya

The plant takes its name from the extremely large petals of the peripheral flowers of the umbel, which consists of up to 12 rays of white flowers; this characteristic makes it easily identifiable. The leaves are deeply divided with ovate lobes. Found in olive groves, fields, and on roadsides.

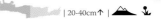 | 20-40cm↑ |

UMBELLIFERAE

1 2 3 4 5 6 7 8 9 10 11 12

Pimpinella tragium subsp. *depressa* (DC.) Tutin ●
Pimpinella tragium ssp. depressa

A small prostrate, perennial with a branching stem which is woody at the base. The leaves are deeply divided with toothed lobes. The umbel consists of white or pink flowers. The plant is endemic and found in stony places in the mountain and alpine zone of the three great massifs of Crete.

 | 10-30cm → |

Smyrnium olusatrum L.
Alexanders

A biennial, aromatic plant with a ridged, hollow stem and large leaves that are trilobate or consist of three leaflets which have thin teeth on the lips. The flowers are yellow, in umbels with up to 18 rays. Found in abandoned fields, olive groves, and ditches.

| 0,5-1m ↑ |

Smyrnium rotundifolium D.C.
Smyrnium rotundifolium

This is also a biennial, with a ridged but not hollow stem; the upper leaves are round and periblastic, making the plant easy to recognize. The flowers are yellow, in umbels which have up to 12 rays. Found in olive groves, thickets, and in dry locations.

| 30-60cm ↑ |

Tordylium apulum L.
Tordylium

A plant with a ridged stem and downy leaves, the lower ones heart-shaped, toothed or trilobate, the upper ones ribbon-like. The flowers are small and white; only one petal of each peripheral flower is larger. The very aromatic leaves give a special flavour to salads. Found in stony locations, olive groves, and fields.

| 10-50cm ↑ |

UMBELLIFERAE

1 2 3 4 5 6 7 8 9 10 11 12

Crithmum maritimum L.
Rock samphire

This is an annual plant with branching stems. The fleshy leaves are elongated and of a characteristic grey colour. The flowers are white in a dense umbel. The leaves, which are edible, are collected before flowering and preserved in salt. Found on cliffs, walls and sands, always near the sea.

| 20-40cm ↑ |

VALERIANACEAE

1 2 3 4 5 6 7 8 9 10 11 12

Centranthus calcitrapae Dufr.
Centranthus calciptrapae

A small, annual, grassy herbaceous plant with an erect stem. The upper leaves are deeply-divided, the lower ones larger and deeply toothed. The small white or pink flowers, in contrast to those of the other members of the family, have a short spur and grow in a dense, terminal fan. The strange name likens the plant to the Roman weapon known as the 'calcitrapa' which hindered the movement of infantry. The plant is found more often in western Crete.

| 10-40cm ↑ |

VALERIANACEAE

1 2 3 4 5 6 7 8 9 10 11 12

Centranthus ruber (L.) DC.
Red valerian

This very beautiful, grey-green plant which can often be seen in gardens and in pots has erect stems with wide, opposite, entire leaves that are sharply pointed and can reach a length of 12cm. The lower leaves have a little stalk while the upper ones are stalk-less. The small, tubular, pink flowers have a five-lobed corolla and a long, slender spur, and grow in a dense cluster. Found in rocky places and on slopes.

| 30-80cm ↑ |

Centranthus sieberii HELDR.
Centranthus sieberii

VALERIANACEAE

1	2	3	4	5	6	7	8	9	10	11	12

A rare plant, endemic to the White Mountains. It has erect stems and lanceolate leaves, concave and with dark margins. The flowers resemble those of *C. ruber* but have a longer spur. Found in stony locations in the mountain and alpine zone.

| 30cm ↑ |

Valeriana asarifolia DUFR.
Cretan valerian

VALERIANACEAE

1	2	3	4	5	6	7	8	9	10	11	12

This is an endemic valerian with a strong, erect stem and distinguished its lower leaves which are long-stalked, kidney-shaped, and slightly toothed, while the upper leaves are deeply divided. The white or pink flowers grow in a dense, head-shaped cluster. Found in rocky places and in phrygana.

 | 20-50cm ↑ |

Vitex agnus castus L.
Chaste tree

VERBENACEAE

1	2	3	4	5	6	7	8	9	10	11	12

An aromatic bush with strong, pliable branches. This characteristic gave the name to the genus; the branches had many uses in the past, the most common of which was basket-making (Latin *vitor* = basket-maker). The bluish-white flowers develop in whorls which form a beautiful, long ear-like spike. The two words in the name of this genus, *agnós* (Greek) and *castus* (Latin) mean the same (chaste) and it is no coincidence that this plant is considered to be anaphrodisiac and sedative. Found in ravines and gorges.

| 1-3m ↑ |

VIOLACEAE

| 1 | 2 | 3 | 4 | 5 | 6 | 7 | 8 | 9 | 10 | 11 | 12 |

Viola fragrans SIEBER ●
Viola fragrans

The beautiful violets or wild
pansies are distinguished
by their flowers with five
petals - two pairs of similar
petals while the fifth protrudes
behind, forming a spur.
V. fragrans has lanceolate leaves
and yellow, white or violet flowers. Found in stony locations
in the subalpine and alpine zone of the
mountains of Crete.

| 5-30cm ↑ |

VIOLACEAE

| 1 | 2 | 3 | 4 | 5 | 6 | 7 | 8 | 9 | 10 | 11 | 12 |

Viola scorpiuroides Coss.
Viola scorpiuroides

A phrygano plant which
originates from
North Africa. It is a
perennial with a woody
stem and inverse-
ovate, downy leaves.
The flowers are fragrant,
up to 1cm in size, yellow and with two
characteristic black spots. It has been
characterised as rare and prefers stony
locations near the sea.

| 10-30cm ↑ |

AGAVACEAE

| 1 | 2 | 3 | 4 | 5 | 6 | 7 | 8 | 9 | 10 | 11 | 12 |

Agave americana L.
Century plant

A plant which originates from Mexico but
has become acclimatized to Greece and
the whole of the Mediterranean area.
The leaves are arranged in a rosette, grey,
large, fleshy and channelled, up to 2
metres long; they are very spiny on the
lips and tip. The agave flowers only once,
when it has reached an age of at least 10
ten years; thereafter it dies. The spike is
large on an impressive stalk up to 6 metres in height, with many flower-bearing stems and yellow flowers. Found in
hedges and on the sides of roads.

| 1-3m ↑ |

Narcissus serotinus L.
Narcissus serotinus

AMARYLLIDACEAE

| 1 | 2 | 3 | 4 | 5 | 6 | 7 | 8 | 9 | 10 | 11 | 12 |

The autumn narcissus is a delicate plant with white flowers whose diameter does not exceed 3cm. The internal corona is yellow, and very small. The stem is slender, cylindrical and 20-30cm long. The leaves are usually absent or produced after flowering. Found in stony places, olive groves and loose thickets.

| 10-30cm ↑ |

Narcissus tazetta L.
Bunch-flowered narcissus

AMARYLLIDACEAE

| 1 | 2 | 3 | 4 | 5 | 6 | 7 | 8 | 9 | 10 | 11 | 12 |

This is perhaps the most fragrant of all the narcissi, known locally in Greece as 'manousáki'; it is avidly collected and sold in bunches on the open market stalls. It has a stout cylindrical stem, and greyish-green leaves with an angular ridge and a length equal to that of the stem. The perianth is white, 3-4cm in diameter, with an internal yellow corona, up to 5 mm in height. There are up to 12 nodding flowers. Found in damp locations.

| 20-50cm ↑ |

Pancratium maritimum L.
Sea daffodil

AMARYLLIDACEAE

| 1 | 2 | 3 | 4 | 5 | 6 | 7 | 8 | 9 | 10 | 11 | 12 |

This is one of the most beautiful of wild flowers and decorates the beaches every summer. It is a perennial, herbaceous plant that grows from a bulb; its leaves are large and ribbon-like, longer than the stem, and have already withered by the time of flowering. The new leaves appear at the beginning of winter. The flowers are large, funnel-shaped, 3-15 in every umbel, fragrant and white. The characteristic fruits resemble pieces of charcoal; they are light in weight and float on the sea, which disperses them along the shore. The beauty of this plant inspired Minoan artists, who depicted it in the palace of Knossos.

| 20-60cm ↑ |

AMARYLLIDACEAE ***Sternbergia greuteriana*** Kamari & Artelari ●

| 1 | 2 | 3 | 4 | 5 | 6 | 7 | 8 | 9 | 10 | 11 | 12 |

Sternbergia greuteriana

This plant is endemic to Crete; it is the smallest of the three types of sternbergia found on the island. It has yellow flowers; the tepals have rather rounded edges. The elongated leaves have a characteristic line down the middle and appear at the same time as the flowers. Found in stony places and phrygana, more often in eastern Crete.

| 10-30cm ↑ |

AMARYLLIDACEAE ***Sternbergia lutea*** (L.) Ker-Gawl. ex Spreng.

| 1 | 2 | 3 | 4 | 5 | 6 | 7 | 8 | 9 | 10 | 11 | 12 |

Common sternbergia

Its flower resembling that of a crocus, *S. lutea* is a perennial herbaceous plant that grows from a bulb. It has lanceolate, elongated, narrow leaves which develop during flowering. The flowers are yellow, with a membrane-like spathe at their base and a perianth divided into 6 lanceolate tepals up to 6cm in length. There are 6 yellow anthers. Found in shady, stony places, olive groves etc. It is often cultivated as a decorative plant.

| 10-30cm ↑ |

AMARYLLIDACEAE ***Sternbergia sicula*** Ten.

| 1 | 2 | 3 | 4 | 5 | 6 | 7 | 8 | 9 | 10 | 11 | 12 |

Sternbergia sicula

This is the most common of the sternbergias. It resembles *S. greuteriana* but has tepals that are pointed at the tip and leaves which appear after flowering. Found in stony places, olive groves, and phrygana. Like the other species, it flowers in the autumn.

| 10-30cm ↑ |

Arisarum vulgare Targ.-Tozz.
Friar's cowl

ARACEAE

| 1 | 2 | 3 | 4 | 5 | 6 | 7 | 8 | 9 | 10 | 11 | 12 |

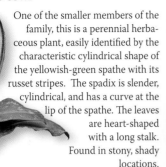

One of the smaller members of the family, this is a perennial herbaceous plant, easily identified by the characteristic cylindrical shape of the yellowish-green spathe with its russet stripes. The spadix is slender, cylindrical, and has a curve at the lip of the spathe. The leaves are heart-shaped with a long stalk. Found in stony, shady locations.

| 20-40cm ↑ |

Arum alpinum Schott & Kotschy
Arum alpinum

ARACEAE

| 1 | 2 | 3 | 4 | 5 | 6 | 7 | 8 | 9 | 10 | 11 | 12 |

14 species of arum are found in Greece. *A. alpinum* prefers higher altitudes – hence its name. It has an oblong green spathe and a slender spadix. The leaves are large and dart-shaped, with a long stalk. It has almost no aroma, and is found singly or in small colonies, normally hidden by bushes.

| 20-40cm ↑ |

Arum concinnatum Schott
Arum concinnatum

ARACEAE

| 1 | 2 | 3 | 4 | 5 | 6 | 7 | 8 | 9 | 10 | 11 | 12 |

This is the most common arum, found in large populations and preferring shaded places and olive groves. The triangular, dart-like leaves appear very early. The spathe is large, yellow or yellow-green, often with violet shading on the lips. The spadix is yellow and much shorter than the spathe.

| 30cm ↑ |

ARACEAE

| 1 | 2 | 3 | 4 | 5 | 6 | 7 | 8 | 9 | 10 | 11 | 12 |

Arum creticum Boiss. & Heldr. ●
Cretan arum

This is perhaps the most beautiful *arum* to be found in Greece. The spathe is a brilliant yellow colour, bending at the tip, and the spadix deep yellow and longer than the spathe. The leaves are large and dart-shaped, often slightly billowy. It usually has a sweet and pleasing aroma, more rarely a slightly rank one. The plant is endemic to Crete and Karpathos, and often occurs in large groups.

| 20- 50cm ↑ |

ARACEAE

| 1 | 2 | 3 | 4 | 5 | 6 | 7 | 8 | 9 | 10 | 11 | 12 |

Arum idaeum Coustur. & Gand ●
Arum idaeum

This beautiful little *arum* is easily recognised by its whitish-green spathe and blackish-purple spadix which does not protrude from the spathe. The leaves are dart-like, and impressively large. During flowering it produces an almost pleasant scent. It is endemic to Crete, and prefers high altitudes. Found beneath cypress and oak trees, often amidst thickets of *Berberis cretica*.

| 20-40cm ↑ |

ARACEAE

| 1 | 2 | 3 | 4 | 5 | 6 | 7 | 8 | 9 | 10 | 11 | 12 |

Biarum davisii Turrill ●
Cretan biarum

This rare, strange little plant with its barrel-like shape is endemic to Crete and was identified relatively recently. The spathe is cream-coloured with white spots, closed and ovoid-cylindrical, with a height which rarely exceeds 5cm. The spadix is funnel-like, and slender at the end which protrudes from the spathe. It flowers in the autumn, the leaves being produced at quite a late stage. It has no aroma. In the past, it was used on Crete to induce abortion.

| 5-10cm ↑ |

Dracunculus vulgaris Schott
Dragon arum, Great dragon

ARACEAE

1 2 3 4 5 6 7 8 9 10 11 12

An impressive plant, with a height which often exceeds 1 metre. The spathe is lanceolate, purple on the inside and yellowish-green on the outside. The spadix is slender, long and purple, but shorter than the spathe. The leaves are large, deeply cut and wavy with white spots. During the flowering period, the plant emits a strong, rank odour which attracts flies. Found on roadsides and in abandoned fields.

| 0,50-1.30m ↑ |

Sesleria doerfleri Hayek
Sesleria doerfleri

GRAMINAE

1 2 3 4 5 6 7 8 9 10 11 12

A rare grass which is endemic to Crete and found in the side walls of gorges in the western part of the island. It has numerous leaves, ribbon-like and typically with a white vein in the middle, and tiny flowers in a spike on a long, thin flower-stalk.

| 20-50cm ↑ |

Tamus communis L.
Black bryony

DIOSCOREACEAE

1 2 3 4 5 6 7 8 9 10 11 12

A perennial, climbing, herbaceous plant with a tuberous root and annual stems. The leaves are heart-shaped, smooth and with a long stalk. The flowers are male and female on different plants (unisexual), small and greenish-yellow, the male flowers in a thick raceme, the female flowers more loosely arranged. The seed is a little red berry. Despite the fact that the plant is poison-ous, the tender stems are considered an excel-lent dish after a procedure has been followed in which they are boiled and the water changed. The plant is used as a purgative in folk medicine. Found in thickets and shady locations.

| 30-60cm ↑ |

GRAMINEAE

`1 2 3 4 5 6 7 8 9 10 11 12`

Ammophila arenaria (L.) LINK
Marram grass

This little arenaceous plant which has chosen sand as its biotope, is not, of course, interesting because of its flower, which looks like a corn-ear, but for the beautiful clumps in which it develops on the sand dunes. It is a very important plant where the stability of this biotope is concerned, since its network of roots holds the sandy soil together. The name comes from the Greek words 'fílos' and 'ámmos', meaning 'lover of sand', and refers very aptly to its preferred habit.

| 0.40-1.20m ↑ |

IRIDACEAE

`1 2 3 4 5 6 7 8 9 10 11 12`

Crocus boryi GAY ●
Crocus boryi

A dead-white flower, yellow at the base. The stigmas are yellowish-orange, torn into fine threads, and shorter than the perianth. The anthers are white, shorter than, or the same length as, the stigmas. The leaves are linear and narrow, reaching to the height of the flowers. Found in stony places, on slopes, and in olive groves.

| 10-20cm ↑ |

IRIDACEAE

`1 2 3 4 5 6 7 8 9 10 11 12`

Crocus cartwrightianus HERB. ●
Greek saffron crocus, Wild saffron crocus

This is the progenitor of the cultivated crocus. At the beginning of the 19th century, J. Cartwright, a British consul at Constantinople, sent a sample of this plant from Tenos to the botanist W. Herbert, who identified the new species and as a consolation to Cartwright gave his name to the plant. The flowers are mauve with dark veining, and the anthers yellow. The stigmas are much larger than the perianth and thus distinguish the plant. Found in stony locations.

| 5-15cm ↑ |

Crocus laevigatus BORY & CHAUB.
Crocus laevigatus

IRIDACEAE

| 1 | 2 | 3 | 4 | 5 | 6 | 7 | 8 | 9 | 10 | 11 | 12 |

This is the most widely distributed of the crocuses and has a long tube and parts of the perianth which are white or slightly mauve, each with three violet lines on the outside; more rarely it is completely white. The anthers are white and the stigmas yellow, torn into thin threads a little shorter than, or of equal length with, the perianth. The leaves have a light-coloured ridge at the centre, and develop during the flowering period. Found in stony places, on slopes, and in forests.

| 5-15cm ↑ |

Crocus oreocreticus B.L. BURTT
Crocus oreocreticus

IRIDACEAE

| 1 | 2 | 3 | 4 | 5 | 6 | 7 | 8 | 9 | 10 | 11 | 12 |

This crocus is endemic to the mountains of Crete, hence its name *'oreocreticus'*, although it is not found in the White Mountains. It greatly resembles *C. cartwrightianus*, but has much shorter stigmas and is darker. Found in stony locations.

| 5-15cm ↑ |

Crocus sieberi ssp. *sieberi* GAY
Crocus sieberi ssp. sieberi

IRIDACEAE

| 1 | 2 | 3 | 4 | 5 | 6 | 7 | 8 | 9 | 10 | 11 | 12 |

This crocus is endemic to the White Mountains and many little outcrops are covered in it during springtime. It has a white perianth with mauve areas on the outside of three of its parts, and a yellow throat. The anthers are yellow and the stigmas orange, entire and with a flat tip. There are more than five leaves, which have a light-coloured ridge in the centre and are the same length as the flowers. Found in stony locations and meadows, often amongst bushes.

| 10-15cm ↑ |

IRIDACEAE

| 1 | 2 | 3 | 4 | 5 | 6 | 7 | 8 | 9 | 10 | 11 | 12 |

Crocus tournefortii GAY ●
Crocus tournefortii

This is one of the most beautiful of the Greek crocuses. The perianth is of light pinkish-mauve shades and the throat yellow. The anthers are white and the stigmas yellow, divided into many threads, and longer than the flower. The leaves are narrow with a white ridge at the centre. Found in stony places and olive groves.

| 5-15cm ↑ |

IRIDACEAE

| 1 | 2 | 3 | 4 | 5 | 6 | 7 | 8 | 9 | 10 | 11 | 12 |

Gladiolus italicus MILLER
Field gladiolus

This is the hyacinth of antiquity, one of the most beautiful wild flowers in the Greek landscape. The strong stem grows from a corm and reaches up to 80cm in height. It has 3-5 leaves, slightly shorter than the stem, with a width of up to 2cm. The flowers are pink, up to 10 in number, on an ear-like spike. It is a very decorative plant and avidly collected for that reason. Found in cultivated fields, olive groves, and meadows.

| 40-80cm ↑ |

IRIDACEAE

| 1 | 2 | 3 | 4 | 5 | 6 | 7 | 8 | 9 | 10 | 11 | 12 |

Gynandriris monophylla BOISS. & HELDR.
Gynandriris monophylla

This is undoubtedly the smallest of the irises with a perianth which does not exceed 2cm. The flowers are usually light blue or violet, the three external parts with a yellow fleck surrounded by white. There is only one leaf – hence the name; the latter is dart-shaped with a length which can reach to 30cm. Found in stony locations and phrygana. The name of this genus originates from the Greek words 'gyní' and 'ándras' ('woman and man'), and refers to the reproductive organs of the plant - the style and stamens - which are joined.

| 5-10cm ↑ |

Gynandriris sisyrinchium (L.) Parl.
Barbary nut

IRIDACEAE

| 1 | 2 | 3 | 4 | 5 | 6 | 7 | 8 | 9 | 10 | 11 | 12 |

This plant grows from a bulb, and is a perennial with flowers similar to those of *G. monophylla* but larger, with a diameter of up to 5cm; they have a short life. There is a fleck on the external parts of the perianth, white or yellow, with violet stippling.

The stems are erect with 1-6 flowers and dart-shaped leaves, fluted and with a length that can reach to 50cm. Found in fields and phrygana. The name originates from Theophrastus and probably refers to the membranous spathe, since the ancient Greek word for the leather *chiton* or tunic was *sísurna*.

| 10-40cm ↑

Hermodactylus tuberosus (L.) Miller
Snake's head or Widow iris

IRIDACEAE

| 1 | 2 | 3 | 4 | 5 | 6 | 7 | 8 | 9 | 10 | 11 | 12 |

A plant resembling the iris. It has an erect stem, square in cross-section, with leaves which are a little longer. There is only one flower, yellowish-green with the edges of the external parts of the perianth a velvety mauve. Found in stony places, olive groves, phrygana and fields.

| 20-40cm ↑

● *Iris cretensis* Poir. / syn. *Iris unguicularis* ssp. *cretensis*
Iris cretensis

IRIDACEAE

| 1 | 2 | 3 | 4 | 5 | 6 | 7 | 8 | 9 | 10 | 11 | 12 |

The Cretan iris is a perennial with short stems and many straight, narrow leaves which resemble grass. It is one of the most beautiful irises. It forms clumps with many violet flowers which bear impressive white and yellow patterns. Found in open, stony locations, in phrygana, and on slopes.

| 20-40cm ↑

IRIDACEAE

| 1 | 2 | 3 | 4 | 5 | 6 | 7 | 8 | 9 | 10 | 11 | 12 |

Iris germanica L.
Iris germanica

A perennial plant with a strong stem that can reach to 1 metre in height. It has large leaves, sword-like and slightly shorter than the stem. The flower is fragrant, up to 10cm, blue-violet with yellow stripes in the centre and white hairs. It is widely cultivated as a decorative plant, often self-sowing.

| 060-1,5m ↑ |

IRIDACEAE

| 1 | 2 | 3 | 4 | 5 | 6 | 7 | 8 | 9 | 10 | 11 | 12 |

Iris pseudacorus L.
Yellow flag

This is a tall perennial with leaves that reach the same height as the stem. The flowers are large and yellow, with the external parts of the perianth much larger than the internal ones. The name refers to *Acorus calamus*, with which it is often confused, since its leaves are similar and it prefers the same biotopes. Found in marshes and damp places.

| 0,5-1m ↑ |

IRIDACEAE

| 1 | 2 | 3 | 4 | 5 | 6 | 7 | 8 | 9 | 10 | 11 | 12 |

Romulea bulbocodium (L.) SEBAST. & MAURI
Romulea bulbocodium

This beautiful plant, which grows from a bulb and resembles the crocus, is easily differentiated by the existence of a flower-stem (not found in the crocus) and the absence of a white line on its narrow leaves. The flowers are up to 3cm in diameter with lanceolate, white tepals, a yellow throat and violet 'brush-strokes'. Found in stony locations and phrygana.

| 5-15cm ↑ |

Romulea linaresii ssp. *graeca* Parl.

Romulea linaresii ssp. graeca

IRIDACEAE

This plant is smaller than R. bulbocodium, with only few leaves (3-5) and a violet flower with a dark-coloured throat. In contrast to *R. bulbocodium* it has stamens which are longer than the pistil. Found in stony locations. The occurrence of this plant on Crete was only recently verified.

| 5-15cm ↑ |

Allium ampeloprasum L.

Wild leek, great round-headed garlic

LILIACEAE

The wild leek is a tall plant with narrow leaves, toothed near the stem, becoming narrower towards the tip. The umbel is up to 8cm in diameter with a multitude of pinkish-red flowers and a strong aroma of garlic. The stamens are shorter than the tepals. It is considered to be the progenitor of the cultivated leek. Usually found in abandoned fields and on roadsides.

| 50-150cm ↑ |

● *Allium callimischon* ssp. *haemostictum* Stern

Allium callimischon ssp. haemostictum

LILIACEAE

A very beautiful, perennial plant of the autumn, with fluted, linear leaves which have already withered by the time of flowering. The dark red spots on the white tepals are very characteristic and have given the subspecies its name (from the Greek words for 'blood' and 'spot'). It prefers stony locations and phrygana and is probably endemic to Crete.

| 10-30cm ↑ |

LILIACEAE

1 2 3 4 5 6 7 8 9 10 11 12

Allium neapolitanum Cyr.
Naples garlic

This has a characteristic triangular stem with one ridge slightly less angular than the other two, and 2-3 smooth leaves. The umbel is loose and up to 10cm in diameter, with white flowers on long stalks. The stamens are shorter than the tepals. The plant is common, with a very wide distribution.

| 20-50cm ↑ | 🏔 🌱 🏵

LILIACEAE

1 2 3 4 5 6 7 8 9 10 11 12

Allium nigrum L.
Allium nigrum

A perennial with leaves that are long and have a width of up to 8cm. The umbel is globular with a diameter of up to 10cm, containing many pink or white flowers with green veining on the outer side. The stamens are a little shorter than the tepals. Found in fields, olive groves, and on roadsides.

| 40-100cm ↑ | 🏔 🌱 🏵

LILIACEAE

1 2 3 4 5 6 7 8 9 10 11 12

Allium roseum L.
Rose garlic

This very beautiful *Allium* has 2-5 fluted leaves that are smooth and slightly toothed. The umbel is globular and up to 7cm with many (up to 30) pink flowers on short stalks. The stamens are longer than the tepals. Found in fields, ditches, and on roadsides.

| 50-80cm ↑ | 🏔

Allium rubrovittatum Boiss. & Heldr.
Allium rubrovittatum

1 2 3 4 5 6 7 8 9 10 11 12

This little wild onion is a perennial with very narrow, linear leaves whose width is almost twice that of the stem. The flowers occur in a dense, ovoid or hemispherical umbel with white tepals which bear red stippling – a characteristic which gives the plant its name. Found in stony places.

| 10-20cm ↑ |

Allium subhirsutum L.
Allium subhirsutum

1 2 3 4 5 6 7 8 9 10 11 12

A plant resembling *A. neapolitanum* but generally smaller in size. Another difference is that it has a cylindrical stem and leaves that are slightly hairy at the lips – hence the name. Found in stony places, on roadsides, in fields, and on slopes.

| 20-40cm ↑ |

Allium tardans Greuter & Zahar.
Allium tardans

1 2 3 4 5 6 7 8 9 10 11 12

As its name suggests, this plant flowers in the autumn. The bell-shaped flowers are arranged in a lax umbel; the peripheral flowers are rather nodding. The tepals are yellowish-pink with dark stipples. Found in stony places and in phrygana.
A. chamaespathum, which flowers during the same period, has whitish-green cylindrical flowers, in a rather spherical umbel.

| 10-30cm ↑ |

LILIACEAE

1 2 3 4 5 6 7 8 9 10 11 12

Androcymbium rechingeri Greuter ●

Androcymbium rechingeri

This beautiful, endemic little lily flowers in the midst of winter. It has a very short stem and elongated, lanceolate, smooth leaves up to 15cm in length. The flowers have a diameter of 3-5cm, with lanceolate tepals, white with pink veining. It is considered to be among the rarest plants in Greece, found in sandy locations on the little islet of Elafónisos and at Falásarna in western Crete.

| 5-10cm ↑ |

LILIACEAE

1 2 3 4 5 6 7 8 9 10 11 12

Asparagus aphyllus L.

Asparagus aphyllus

A spiny, often climbing and much-branched phrygano plant in which the leaves have been replaced by spiny, infertile branchlets which grow in clusters. The flowers are yellowish-green, fleshy and in small groups. The wild asparagus is edible; the tender tips of the stems are gathered and considered a choice dish. Found in olive groves, hedgerows, and phrygana.

| 0.50-1m ↑ |

LILIACEAE

1 2 3 4 5 6 7 8 9 10 11 12

Asphodeline liburnica (Scop.) Rchb.

Asphodeline liburnica

A delicate, perennial plant with narrow, linear leaves which reach to the middle of the stem. The flowers are yellow, almost similar to those of *A. lutea* but arranged in a much looser spike. Found in stony locations and abandoned fields.

| 20-60cm ↑ |

WILD FLOWERS OF CRETE 165

Asphodeline lutea (L.) Rᴄʜʙ.
Yellow asphodel

LILIACEAE

| 1 | 2 | 3 | 4 | 5 | 6 | 7 | 8 | 9 | 10 | 11 | 12 |

A perennial plant with an erect stem and many narrow leaves along almost its whole length; this is a characteristic which differentiates it from the asphodel. The flowers are yellow in a dense raceme at the tip of the stem. The plant often forms large communities and it is in one such meadow, in Hades, according to Homer, that the souls of the Dead are gathered. The tender stems of the plant are edible. Found in infertile, stony locations and in phrygana.

| 0.50-1.20m ↑ | 🏔 🌿 ⏚

Asphodelus aestivus Bʀᴏᴛ.
Common asphodel

LILIACEAE

| 1 | 2 | 3 | 4 | 5 | 6 | 7 | 8 | 9 | 10 | 11 | 12 |

This is the most common of the asphodels. It is a perennial with a cylindrical, hollow stem, branching at the tip. The leaves are elongated and triangular; in contrast to those of *Asphodeline*, they are all concentrated at the base of the stem. The flowers have white tepals with russet veining in the centre, and are in terminal racemes. Found in infertile, stony locations, often in large populations.

| 0.50-1.25m ↑ | 🏔 🌿

Asphodelus fistulosus L.
Hollow-leaved asphodel

LILIACEAE

| 1 | 2 | 3 | 4 | 5 | 6 | 7 | 8 | 9 | 10 | 11 | 12 |

A more delicate plant than *A. aestivus*, with many slender, hollow (empty) stems. The leaves are narrow and straight, all concentrated at the base of the stem. The flowers are white or slightly shaded with pink, with brownish veining at the centre of the tepals, in a loose raceme. The fruits, as in the other varieties of *Asphodelus* and *Asphodeline*, are round berries. Found in barren, stony locations.

| 20-60cm ↑ | 🏔 🌿

LILIACEAE

Bellevalia brevipedicellata Lapeyr. ●
Bellevalia brevipedicellata

| 1 | 2 | 3 | 4 | 5 | 6 | 7 | 8 | 9 | 10 | 11 | 12 |

This little plant which resembles muscari (grape hyacinth) is endemic to Crete and found only in the north-west tip of the island at low altitudes. The leaves are fluted, billowy and have a length of up to 20 cm. The white flowers have pink lobes and grow in a long, cylindrical or pyramid-shaped raceme. Found in stony places and phrygana, near the sea. The similar-looking *B. sitiaca* is also endemic and found in eastern Crete.

| 5-20cm ↑ |

LILIACEAE

Chionodoxa nana Boiss. & Heldr. / syn. *Scilla nana* ●
Chionodoxa nana

| 1 | 2 | 3 | 4 | 5 | 6 | 7 | 8 | 9 | 10 | 11 | 12 |

This little plant with its blindingly blue flower has perhaps the most beautiful name in the world – and this is not by pure chance, since it often appears like a surprise from out of the snow. It grows from a bulb and has a slender stem, up to 20cm, and elongated, lanceolate and fluted leaves. The flowers are blue, white at the centre, and have a diameter of up to 4cm. Found in the mountain and alpine zone in the mountains of Crete.

| 5-20cm ↑ |

*C*LILIACEAE

Colchicum cretense Greuter ●
Colchicum cretense

| 1 | 2 | 3 | 4 | 5 | 6 | 7 | 8 | 9 | 10 | 11 | 12 |

The Cretan colchicum is a dwarf plant with flowers ranging from pink to almost white, and tepals up to 2cm. The leaves appear after flowering, which takes place in autumn. The plant is endemic to the great mountain massifs of Crete.

| 5-10cm ↑ |

Colchicum macrophyllum B.L. Burtt
Colchicum macrophyllum

LILIACEAE

| 1 | 2 | 3 | 4 | 5 | 6 | 7 | 8 | 9 | 10 | 11 | 12 |

One of the most beautiful of the colchicums, with large, elegant flowers decorated with pink spots like a mosaic. It flowers early in autumn and prefers fertile, shaded soil in pine forests and olive groves. The tepals are more than 5cm long. The leaves are very large, up to 30cm – hence the name – and are produced in spring.

| 10-30cm ↑ |

Colchicum pusillum Sieber
Colchicum pusillum

LILIACEAE

| 1 | 2 | 3 | 4 | 5 | 6 | 7 | 8 | 9 | 10 | 11 | 12 |

A very small plant with flowers in a variety of pink tones; up to 4 flowers grow from every bulb. The anthers are yellow. The lanceolate leaves appear together with the flowers in autumn. Found in open stony locations and in loose phrygana thickets.

C. cupani is similar, with a distribution that reaches as far as Epirus. It differs in its leaves, which are broader, and in the anthers, which are darker.

| 5-10cm ↑ |

Fritillaria messanensis Raf.
Fritillaria messanensis

LILIACEAE

| 1 | 2 | 3 | 4 | 5 | 6 | 7 | 8 | 9 | 10 | 11 | 12 |

A delicately-built plant with very narrow greyish leaves, the lower ones arranged singly and alternate, and the upper ones in whorls of three. There are 1-2 flowers, more or less similar to those of *F. graeca* but with stronger blazon patterns and lips slightly turned outwards. The anthers are yellow. Usually found in open phrygana.

| 15-40cm ↑ |

LILIACEAE

| 1 | 2 | 3 | 4 | 5 | 6 | 7 | 8 | 9 | 10 | 11 | 12 |

Gagea graeca L.
Gagea graeca

This is distinguished from other varieties of gagea by its white, bell-shaped flower. It is a perennial with slender, well-bent stems and dart-shaped leaves, most of them basal. There are up to three flowers, six-part and with dark veining. Found in areas of phrygana and stony places.

 | 5-25cm ↑ |

LILIACEAE

| 1 | 2 | 3 | 4 | 5 | 6 | 7 | 8 | 9 | 10 | 11 | 12 |

Gagea peduncularis (J. & Presl) Pasch.
Gagea peduncularis

A small, perennial, downy plant with short stems. The upper leaves are lanceolate, the lower leaves – of which there are always 2 – are linear and fluted. The flowers are yellow, greenish on the exterior, solitary and have a diameter of up to 2.5cm. Found in thickets, phrygana, and open stony locations.

Many other species, such as *G. bohemica*, are similar but exhibit little differences in their leaves and the shape of the tepals.

 | 5-15cm ↑ |

LILIACEAE

| 1 | 2 | 3 | 4 | 5 | 6 | 7 | 8 | 9 | 10 | 11 | 12 |

Muscari commutatum Guss.
Dark grape hyacinth

The Muscari are perennial, herbaceous plants with all their leaves concentrated at the base and flowers which are usually ovoid or cylindrical in shape, narrowing towards the toothed lip, and arranged in a terminal raceme. *M. commutatum* has linear, fluted leaves, and a dense flower-spike, ovoid with dark blue-violet flowers. Found in stony locations, pine forests and on the slopes at the sides of roads.

 | 10-20cm ↑ |

Muscari comosum (L.) MILL.
Tassel hyacinth

LILIACEAE

| 1 | 2 | 3 | 4 | 5 | 6 | 7 | 8 | 9 | 10 | 11 | 12 |

This is the most common of the *Muscari* and has concave leaves that are up to 3cm wide and 40cm long. The lower section of the raceme is loose and consists of brown flowers, while the upper section is denser with blue-violet flowers. The upper flowers are sterile. Found in fields, often in large populations. The bulbs of *M. comosum* constitute an excellent appetizer known as *skordouláki*, especially on Crete.

| 15-50cm ↑ |

Muscari neglectum GUSS. EX TEN. / syn. *M. racemosum*
Common grape hyacinth

LILIACEAE

| 1 | 2 | 3 | 4 | 5 | 6 | 7 | 8 | 9 | 10 | 11 | 12 |

This plant has narrow, cylindrical and ridged leaves which are longer than the stem. The flowers are arranged in a raceme, and are light or dark blue; they more or less resemble those of *M. commutatum*, but have a white, toothed lip. Found in rocky locations and abandoned fields.

| 5-20cm ↑ |

● *Muscari spreitzenhoferi* (OSTERM.) VIERH.
Muscari spreitzenhoferi

LILIACEAE

| 1 | 2 | 3 | 4 | 5 | 6 | 7 | 8 | 9 | 10 | 11 | 12 |

This little muscari is endemic to Crete and found in rocky places from sea level up to the subalpine zone. The leaves are relatively wide and the flowers arranged in a raceme, the upper ones dark blue and sterile, the lower ones brownish-yellow and fertile. The shape of the plant can vary between biotopes.

| 5-20cm ↑ |

| 1 | 2 | 3 | 4 | 5 | 6 | 7 | 8 | 9 | 10 | 11 | 12 |

Ornithogalum creticum ZAHAR. ●

Ornithogalum creticum

A plant which is endemic to the southern Aegean, distinguished both by its colour and by its relatively late flowering period. The flowers are yellow-green; the linear leaves have already withered by the time of flowering. Found in rocky places, on slopes and in phrygana.

| 10-20cm ↑ |

Ornithogalum dictaeum ssp. dictaeum LANDSTRÖM ●

Ornithogalum dictaeum ssp. dictaeum

| 1 | 2 | 3 | 4 | 5 | 6 | 7 | 8 | 9 | 10 | 11 | 12 |

This little, endemic ornithogalum which is found in the White Mountains and on Dikti is distinguished by its almost flat leaves, from which the characteristic white line seen in other, similar varieties is absent.

| 10-20cm ↑ |

| 1 | 2 | 3 | 4 | 5 | 6 | 7 | 8 | 9 | 10 | 11 | 12 |

Ornithogalum exscapum TEN.

Ornithogalum exscapum

A small, almost stemless plant with linear, concave leaves. The flowers have white tepals which are green on the outside with a white border. Found in phrygana and rocky places. The rarer *O. sibthorpii* is similar but its pericarp is oblong in shape.

| 5-10cm ↑ |

Ornithogalum narbonense L. / syn. *O. pyramidale*

Ornithogalum narbonense

LILIACEAE

| 1 | 2 | 3 | 4 | 5 | 6 | 7 | 8 | 9 | 10 | 11 | 12 |

This is the most common of all the ornithogala and can reach a height of up to 60cm. It is distinguished by its typical pyramid-shaped inflorescence, to which another name for the plant refers. The leaves are ribbon-like and remain during the flowering period. The inflorescence contains many flowers which have a diameter of up to 3cm and are flat. Found in phrygana, ditches, fields, and on roadsides.

| 20-60cm ↑ |

Ornithogalum nutans L.

Drooping Star of Bethlehem

LILIACEAE

| 1 | 2 | 3 | 4 | 5 | 6 | 7 | 8 | 9 | 10 | 11 | 12 |

One of the most elegant of the ornithogala and distinguished by its bell-shaped, drooping flowers which give it the name. The leaves are narrow and channelled, the height of the plant. The tepals are up to 3cm with characteristic silver-green colouring which distinguishes this variety from others. Found in fields and phrygana, usually in the mountain zone.

| 20-60cm ↑ |

Ruscus aculeatus L.

Butcher's broom

LILIACEAE

| 1 | 2 | 3 | 4 | 5 | 6 | 7 | 8 | 9 | 10 | 11 | 12 |

This is a beautiful, decorative shrub, which often confuses those who see it because it appears to produce fruits from the leaves. In reality however, what look like leaves are only leaf-shaped, leathery branchlets, barbed at the tip (*aculeus* = barbed).The flowers are stalkless and appear on the branchlets in the spring, to be followed in summer by cherry-like fruits. Found in shaded locations and forested areas.

| 0,5-1m ↑ |

LILIACEAE

1 2 3 4 5 6 7 8 9 10 11 12

Scilla autumnalis L.
Autumn squill

As its name suggests, this little squill flowers in the autumn. It is a perennial plant that grows from a bulb with an erect stem and linear, smooth leaves which appear after flowering, all basal. The flowers are small, 1cm at the most, with slender stalks; they are pink, blue or violet with black anthers. The spike consists of a pyramidal raceme at the end of the stem. Found in rocky locations, on slopes, in phrygana and on roadsides.

| 5-30cm ↑ |

LILIACEAE

1 2 3 4 5 6 7 8 9 10 11 12

Smilax aspera L.
Common smilax

A climbing plant, common in hedgerows and thickets. It has a spiny stem, square in cross-section, and can reach a great height. The leaves are dart- to heart-shaped, smooth and leathery with two tendrils at the base of the leaf-stalk. The flowers are fragrant, light-coloured in shades of pink, yellow and green, in hanging inflorescences. The fruits are red berries arranged in bunches, and very decorative.

| 0,5-15m ↑ → |

LILIACEAE

1 2 3 4 5 6 7 8 9 10 11 12

Tulipa bakeri A.D. HALL ●
Tulipa bakeri

This beautiful tulip covers the fields of the Omalos High Plateau on Crete in spring with its multicoloured flowers. The tepals are 4-5cm in length, yellow at the base, white at the centre and pink at the tip, the latter colour predominating. The anthers are yellow. The leaves are concentrated at the base of the stem, elongated, lanceolate and fluted. The plant is endemic to Crete.

| 20-40cm ↑ |

• *Tulipa cretica* Boiss. & Heldr.
Cretan tulip

The smallest of the Cretan tulips, with a stem which does not exceed 15 cm in length and elongated, fluted leaves at the base of the plant. The perianth is white with pink shading on the external surface. The throat and anthers are yellow. This elegant plant is endemic to Crete and found in phrygana and stony locations.

| 5-15cm ↑ | ▲ ⚓ ◆

• *Tulipa doerfleri* Gand.
Tulipa doerfleri

This endemic tulip is found mainly on the little mountain plateau of 'Yous Kámbos' in central Crete. The petals are 3-4cm, narrowing to a point at the tip; they are red, often with yellow shading on the outside. The anthers are blackish-red, and the leaves narrow, elongated and ridged.

| 10-30cm ↑ | ▲ ⚓ ◆

• *Tulipa goulimyi* Sealy & Turrill
Tulipa goulimyi

This plant is found mainly in the southern Peloponnese and on Kythera. The only population to be found on Crete is located on the Gramvousa Peninsula. *T. goulimyi* bears quite a resemblance to *T. doerfleri*; the colours of the tepals range from orange to dark red. A particular characteristic is presented by its billowy leaves, which make it easily recognizable. Found in phrygana, often near the sea.

| 10-30cm ↑ | ▲ ⚓ ◆

Tulipa saxatilis Sieber ex Sprengel
Rock tulip

| 1 | 2 | 3 | 4 | 5 | 6 | 7 | 8 | 9 | 10 | 11 | 12 |

There are no clear botanical differences between this plant and *T. bakeri*; it differs in the colour of the anthers, which here are black or brown. Found in various biotopes from rocky slopes to uncultivated fields and the sides of streams. It is often met at low altitudes; this also differentiates it from *T. bakeri* which prefers altitudes of above 800 metres.

| 10-30cm ↑ | ⛰ ⚓

Urginea maritima L. (Baker) / syn. *Drimia maritima*
Sea squill

| 1 | 2 | 3 | 4 | 5 | 6 | 7 | 8 | 9 | 10 | 11 | 12 |

A common, widely distributed perennial plant with a large, bulky bulb which can reach up to 15cm in diameter. The leaves are smooth, broad, and lanceolate and appear in spring, while by the middle of summer, shortly before flowering, they have already disappeared. The flower-bearing stem is russet-coloured, erect, slender and leafless. The flowers are very many in number, in a dense elongated spike; the tepals are white with a pink vein. Despite its name, it is found all the way up to the mountain zone in stony and barren locations, phrygana, oak forests and olive groves.

| 0,5-1m ↑ | ⛰ ⚓ ☠ ▆

Aceras anthropophorum (L.) W.T. Aiton
Man orchid

| 1 | 2 | 3 | 4 | 5 | 6 | 7 | 8 | 9 | 10 | 11 | 12 |

A very individual-looking, dainty plant with a dense ear-like inflorescence and flowers with a lip divided into four straight lobes which make it look like a little man – hence its name (*ánthropos*= man, *féro*= to bear). Its colouring varies from russet to greenish-yellow, while the absence of a spur is characteristic. The leaves are concentrated in a rosette at the base of the plant. It is mainly found in phrygana thickets.

| 10-30cm ↑ | ⛰ ⚓

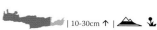

Anacamptis pyramidalis (L.) Rıch.
Pyramidal orchid

ORCHIDACEAE

| 1 | 2 | 3 | 4 | 5 | 6 | 7 | 8 | 9 | 10 | 11 | 12 |

This is one of the more common orchids, and a unique representative of its genus. The name comes from the Greek word *anakámp-to*, meaning 'to turn/bend backwards', and probably refers to the the long, slender spur which is turned upwards. The plant has a slender stem and very characteristic pyramid-shaped flower-spike with white or pink flowers, their lip divided into three equal lobes. The leaves are concentrated at the base and have almost withered by the time of flowering. Usually found in phrygana.

| 15- 40cm ↑ |

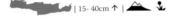

Barlia robertiana (Loısel.) Greuter
Robert's giant orchid

ORCHIDACEAE

| 1 | 2 | 3 | 4 | 5 | 6 | 7 | 8 | 9 | 10 | 11 | 12 |

This orchid is undoubtedly the largest in height, often reaching to over 50cm, with large leaves that are often rolled around the brownish stem. The flowers are arranged in a dense spike in a variety of colours and shades, from red and white to green. The lip is trilobate, often with spotting; the side lobes are undulating, the middle one is divided. Found in phrygana, stony locations, and olive groves.

| 30-70cm ↑ |

• *Cephalanthera cucullata* Boıss. & Heldr.
Hooded cephalanthera

ORCHIDACEAE

| 1 | 2 | 3 | 4 | 5 | 6 | 7 | 8 | 9 | 10 | 11 | 12 |

C. cucullata ia a rare endemic species with a very limited occurrence on the three great mountains of Crete and considered to be threatened with extinction. It does not exceed 30cm in height and is smaller than the other varieties of cephalanthera. It has white or whitish-pink flowers in a relatively dense spike with the bracts covering the flowers like a hood. It has a small spur and is the only cephalanthera to exhibit this characteristic. Found in phrygana, forests and shady, cool locations.

| 10-30cm ↑ |

Dactylorhiza romana (Sebast.) Soó
Roman cuckoo flower, Roman orchid

This has lanceolate leaves concentrated in a rosette at the base of the plant. The flowers may be purple, ochre-white or white and have long spurs which are turned upwards, a characteristic which differentiates the plant from the similar-looking *D. sambucina*. Found in forest clearings, olive groves, thickets and phrygana.

| 10-40cm ↑ |

Epipactis microphylla (Ehrh.) Sw.
Small-leaved helleborine

This dainty orchid has a downy stem and small leaves, which differentiate it from the endemic and rarer *E. cretica* with its larger, broader leaves. The flowers emit the aroma of vanilla; they are small and almost closed with white fleshy swellings on the lip. Found in shady, damp places.

| 10-40cm ↑ |

Himatoglossum samariense C.&A. Alibertis ●
Himantoglossum samariense

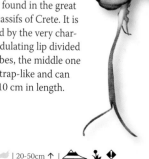

This special and rare endemic orchid, which was only recently identified, is found in the great mountain massifs of Crete. It is distinguished by the very characteristic undulating lip divided into three lobes, the middle one of which is strap-like and can reach up to 10 cm in length.

| 20-50cm ↑ |

Limodorum abortivum (L.) Swartz

ORCHIDACEAE

Violet limodore, violet bird's nest orchid

| 1 | 2 | 3 | 4 | 5 | 6 | 7 | 8 | 9 | 10 | 11 | 12 |

The name of this strange but at the same time impressive, slender-bodied orchid comes from the absence of leaves, which gives the impression that the plant has cast them off. Those few leaves that do exist are small and wrapped on the stem. It has large whitish-violet flowers with spreading sepals and a darker lip, curving downwards. It is usually found in pine forests.

| 30-60cm ↑ |

Neotinea maculata (Desf.) Stearn / syn. *Orchis intacta*

ORCHIDACEAE

Dense-flowering orchid

| 1 | 2 | 3 | 4 | 5 | 6 | 7 | 8 | 9 | 10 | 11 | 12 |

A small, perennial orchid, with leaves in a rosette, the upper ones enclosing the stem. The tiny, anthropomorphic whitish-pink flowers form a dense spike. The sepals and petals form a small dome. The lip is trilobate with the large middle lobe divided at the centre. The flowers, stem and leaves are often spotted, hence the name. Found in pine forests, thickets and phrygana.

| 10-20cm ↑ |

Ophrys apifera Huds.

ORCHIDACEAE

Bee orchid

| 1 | 2 | 3 | 4 | 5 | 6 | 7 | 8 | 9 | 10 | 11 | 12 |

This is the only one of all the Greek Ophrys which is self-pollinating – that is, the anthers touch the stigmatic cavity without the help of insects. The protuberance which turns in on itself below the lip and the large and nose-like pistil column are characteristic. The sepals are almost white with green or pink shading. The terminal lobes of the lip are downy. The plant prefers damp meadows.

| 10-50cm ↑ |

ORCHIDACEAE **_Ophrys ariadnae_** Paulus / syn. _Ophrys cretica_ ssp. _ariadnae_ ●

| 1 | 2 | 3 | 4 | 5 | 6 | 7 | 8 | 9 | 10 | 11 | 12 |

Ariadne's ophrys

This plant is endemic to the southern Aegean. It resembles _O. cretica_ and is also considered to be a subspecies of it (_O. cretica_ ssp. _ariadnae_). The sepals are green, more rarely red, and the petals brown. The lip is dark and trilobate with downy, rounded side lobes. The blazon is violet in colour with a white design in the shape of the letter H, or it can be more elaborate. Found in phrygana.

| 20-30cm ↑ |

ORCHIDACEAE **_Ophrys basilissa_** Alibertis & Reinhard ●

| 1 | 2 | 3 | 4 | 5 | 6 | 7 | 8 | 9 | 10 | 11 | 12 |

Royal orchid

The name of this plant clearly reflects the particular characteristic of the species, i.e. the large size of the lip (up to 3.5 cm). The plant resembles _O. omegaifera_ and is also referred to as a subspecies of the latter (_O. omegaifera_ ssp. _basilissa_). It flowers early and is found in phrygana and olive groves.

| 10-30cm ↑ |

ORCHIDACEAE **_Ophrys bombyliflora_** Link

| 1 | 2 | 3 | 4 | 5 | 6 | 7 | 8 | 9 | 10 | 11 | 12 |

Bumblebee ophrys

The smaller of the _Ophrys_, this is easily identified by its little flower, which does not exceed 2cm, with the rounded brownish central lobe and smaller, downy lateral lobes. The sepals are round, green and a little larger than the lip. The two petals are the same colour, but with a brownish base. Found in phrygana and olive groves.

| 10-25cm ↑ |

Ophrys candica GREUTER, MATTHÄS & RISSE
White ophrys

ORCHIDACEAE

| 1 | 2 | 3 | 4 | 5 | 6 | 7 | 8 | 9 | 10 | 11 | 12 |

A relatively rare orchid with a blazon pattern which resembles marble. The sepals and petals are light pink, the latter very small. The lip is undivided, downy on the edge, with two little humps at the edges of the blazon. At the centre of the lip there is a little protuberance turned upwards, similar to that of *O. episcopalis*. Found in phrygana and areas of sparse forest.

| 20-30cm ↑

● *Ophrys creberrima* PAULUS / syn. *Ophrys fusca* ssp. *creberrima*   ORCHIDACEAE
Creberrima ophrys

| 1 | 2 | 3 | 4 | 5 | 6 | 7 | 8 | 9 | 10 | 11 | 12 |

The classification of the Fusca group over recent years has assigned 4 endemic species to Crete whose recognition is a source of headache. *O. creberrima*, also known as *O. fusca* ssp. *creberrima*, has a three-lobed, dark-coloured lip, often with a yellow design on the lower, downward-folded lips and marked sagging at the base. Found in phrygana, on slopes and in olive groves.

| 5-20cm ↑

● *Ophrys cressa* PAULUS / syn. *Ophrys fusca* ssp. *cressa*
Cressa ophrys

ORCHIDACEAE

| 1 | 2 | 3 | 4 | 5 | 6 | 7 | 8 | 9 | 10 | 11 | 12 |

This plant is larger than *O. creberrima* with a lip of up to 14 mm and lobes which are clearly separated and spread out rather flat. Flowering is late compared with other species – something which makes recognition of the species relatively easy. Found in open phrygana in the semi-mountainous zone.

| 10-25cm ↑

ORCHIDACEAE

1 2 3 4 5 6 7 8 9 10 11 12

Ophrys cretica (Vierh.) E. Nelson ●
Ophrys cretica

Similar to *O. ariadnae* but the width of its stigmatic cavity is greater than that of its height. The sepals are light green with brown shading and the petals are brownish-red. The lip is almost black, trilobate, slightly downy with the side lobes more hairy and rather pointed at the tip. The blazon is violet with a design in the form of the letter H. Found in phrygana and olive groves.

 | 20-30cm ↑ | ⛰ 🌱

ORCHIDACEAE **Ophrys creticola** Paulus / syn. *Ophrys fusca* ssp. *creticola* ●

1 2 3 4 5 6 7 8 9 10 11 12

Creticola ophrys

This fusca which already flowers from January onwards has a larger lip than its cousins since its length reaches up to 18 mm. Its lobes spread out flat with each other, often with a thin, yellow border and a blazon resembling that of *O. iricolor*. Found in open locations and in phrygana.

 | 5-15cm ↑ | ⛰

ORCHIDACEAE

1 2 3 4 5 6 7 8 9 10 11 12

Ophrys episcopalis Poir.
Large-flowered bee ophrys

This plant has an impressive, large and undivided lip with its borders turned slightly upwards and humps at the shoulders, which are very downy. At the centre of the lip there is a large protuberance, also turned upwards. The blazon has a yellowish-green pattern. The sepals and petals are pink. *O. episcopalis* is closely related to the *O. holoserica* of central Europe.

 | 10-40cm ↑ | ⛰ 🌱

Ophrys fleischmannii Hayek
Fleischmann's ophrys

ORCHIDACEAE

| 1 | 2 | 3 | 4 | 5 | 6 | 7 | 8 | 9 | 10 | 11 | 12 |

A small plant which has a very characteristic trilobate, strongly haired brown-black lip with dense, long, white hair. The blazon is downy and bears a wide, white pattern in the shape of the Greek letter 'omega'. It flowers relatively early and is more often found in the eastern part of Crete, usually in phrygana.

| 5-15cm ↑ | 🌱 ◈

Ophrys grigoriana G. & H. Kretzschmar
Ophrys grigoriana

ORCHIDACEAE

| 1 | 2 | 3 | 4 | 5 | 6 | 7 | 8 | 9 | 10 | 11 | 12 |

This ophrys is endemic to Crete and has caused enough confusion to botanists as it is also known as *O. spruneri* ssp. *gregoriana* and *O. sphaciotica*. It bears quite a resemblance to *O. spruneri*, with the difference that it has an impressively large lip and vestigial side lobes; in reality, the lip is undivided. The plant flowers relatively late and has taken its name from the region of Gregorias, where it is most frequently found.

| 10-40cm ↑ | ⛰ 🌱 ◈

Ophrys heldreichii Schelter
Heldreich's ophrys

ORCHIDACEAE

| 1 | 2 | 3 | 4 | 5 | 6 | 7 | 8 | 9 | 10 | 11 | 12 |

This plant has an ovate, three-lobed lip. The middle, large lobe has a raised protuberance and side borders turned inwards, this giving it the ovate appearance. The blazon has a leather-like texture and whitish-yellow pattern. The two lateral lobes have noses, and are hairy with strong humps at their base. The sepals and petals are pink. Very frequent in occurrence, found mainly in phrygana.

| 10-40cm ↑ | ⛰ 🌱

ORCHIDACEAE

| 1 | 2 | 3 | 4 | 5 | 6 | 7 | 8 | 9 | 10 | 11 | 12 |

Ophrys herae HIRTH & SPAETH ●
Hera's ophrys

This little ophrys belongs to the *sphegodes-mammosa* complex of which the various species exhibit indistinct botanical differences; consequently classification is difficult. Here, the undivided, almost round lip is brownish-red and has a diameter of a little over 1cm. It bears a light-coloured blazon in the form of the letter H and two characteristic swellings. Found in phrygana.

 | 15-30cm ↑ | ⚓

ORCHIDACEAE

| 1 | 2 | 3 | 4 | 5 | 6 | 7 | 8 | 9 | 10 | 11 | 12 |

Ophrys iricolor DESF.
Rainbow ophrys

With the impressive, iridescent blue colour of the blazon and its characteristic purple colouring on the lower surface of the lip, this plant is easily recognised. Also characteristic is the little V-shaped groove which is created by the two swellings at the base of the trilobate, downy lip. The sepals are green and the petals are oblong, brownish-pink in colour. Found in phrygana, often beneath bushes.

 | 10-30cm ↑ | ⛰ ⚓

ORCHIDACEAE

| 1 | 2 | 3 | 4 | 5 | 6 | 7 | 8 | 9 | 10 | 11 | 12 |

Ophrys mammosa DESF.
Breasted ophrys

A plant similar in form to *O. herae* but larger. The colours of the flowers recall rather those of *O. spruneri*, while the dark colour in the stigmatic cavity is characteristic. It forms hybrids with the two latter plants and is found in phrygana thickets over the whole of Crete.

 | 20-60cm ↑ | ⛰ ⚓

Ophrys mesaritica Paulus & C.&A. Alibertis

ORCHIDACEAE

Mesara ophrys

| 1 | 2 | 3 | 4 | 5 | 6 | 7 | 8 | 9 | 10 | 11 | 12 |

A rare orchid with a very early flowering period, is found mainly in the Mesara region of Crete. The flower has a dark lip and brilliant blue blazon, becoming greener in the lower part – something which distinguishes it from the very similar *O. iricolor* which in any case flowers much later. Found in bushy phrygana thickets.

| 30-40cm ↑ |

Ophrys omegaifera H. Fleischm.

ORCHIDACEAE

Ophrys omegaifera

| 1 | 2 | 3 | 4 | 5 | 6 | 7 | 8 | 9 | 10 | 11 | 12 |

The lip is brownish-red, downy, and three-lobed with a smooth blazon, lighter in colour, which is edged in white or blue in the manner of the Greek letter 'ω' (omega). The basal groove is missing from the strongly curved lip – this distinguishes it from *O. fusca* which often has the same blazon. The sepals are green and the petals have a russet-coloured, billowy edge.

| 10-40cm ↑ |

Ophrys phryganae J. & P. Devillers-Terschuren

ORCHIDACEAE

Phrygana ophrys

| 1 | 2 | 3 | 4 | 5 | 6 | 7 | 8 | 9 | 10 | 11 | 12 |

The lip is three-lobed and can reach up to 1.5cm. It is distinguished by the yellow border to its pattern, while in the centre it is brownish with a blazon that can take various metallic shades. The sepals are green and the petals small and yellowish-green. The downward turn of the lip at the base of the blazon is characteristic.

| 10-30cm ↑ |

ORCHIDACEAE

1 2 3 4 5 6 7 8 9 10 11 12

Ophrys sicula Tineo
Small yellow ophrys

A plant resembling *O. phryganae* but smaller in size overall and without the characteristic sagging of the lip. This little orchid is common all over the island but because of its size it often goes unnoticed. The two plants replace *O. lutea*, which is widely distributed in the Mediterranean but not found on Crete.

 | 5-20cm ↑ |

ORCHIDACEAE

1 2 3 4 5 6 7 8 9 10 11 12

Ophrys sitiaca Paulus & C.& A. Alibertis ●
Sitia ophrys

A plant identified relatively recently on Crete but also found on a number of islands in the south-east Aegean. The lip recalls that of *O. omegaifera* but bears a characteristic though flatter groove common to the species of the fusca group; this provides a snapshot of the hybrid origin of the plant. It is more often found in the eastern half of Crete, usually in phrygana.

 | 10-20cm ↑ |

ORCHIDACEAE

1 2 3 4 5 6 7 8 9 10 11 12

Ophrys sphegodes ssp. *cretensis* Mill. / syn. *O. cretensis* ●
Early spider orchid

A delicate plant which can reach a height of 50cm. The lip is brownish-red, ovate, and undivided with two little downy humps in place of the lateral lobes. The blazon resembles that of *O. spruneri*. The sepals and petals are green, the latter sometimes brownish.

 | 10-50cm ↑ |

Ophrys spruneri Nyman
Grecian spider orchid

ORCHIDACEAE

| 1 | 2 | 3 | 4 | 5 | 6 | 7 | 8 | 9 | 10 | 11 | 12 |

A very beautiful orchid with impressive colouring. The lip is clearly three-lobed, ovate - as are the smaller side lobes – and downy. The blazon has an intense metallic blue and light mauve device in the form of the letter 'H' which is sometimes interrupted in the middle. At the edge of the lip there is a small russet-coloured protuberance pointing upwards. The sepals are pink, darker on the underside, and the petals are narrow, from red to green in colour. Relatively rare, found in phrygana and olive groves.

| 40cm ↑ |

Ophrys tenthredinifera Willd.
Wasp ophrys, sawfly orchid

ORCHIDACEAE

| 1 | 2 | 3 | 4 | 5 | 6 | 7 | 8 | 9 | 10 | 11 | 12 |

Although a common species, *O. tenthredinifera* is one of the most beautiful orchids. The sepals are pink and the small petals the same colour. The lip is undivided, downy, yellow on the edges and brownish towards the centre, with two little humps on the shoulders and a small, yellow protuberance at the tip which is turned upwards. The blazon is smooth, brownish-red with a light coloured outline, orange at the base. Found in phrygana, open stony locations and thickets.

| 10-45cm ↑ |

Ophrys thriptiensis Paulus / syn. *O. fusca* ssp. *thriptiensis*
Thripti ophrys

ORCHIDACEAE

| 1 | 2 | 3 | 4 | 5 | 6 | 7 | 8 | 9 | 10 | 11 | 12 |

This small member of the fusca group, which flowers very early, is endemic to Mount Thripti in eastern Crete. The lip, which here is almost flat, bears the groove which is characteristic of the group with only the middle lobe turned downwards. The blazon has blue and silver metallic shading. Found at altitudes of above 700 metres, in phrygana and pine forests.

| 5-20cm ↑ |

ORCHIDACEAE

1 2 3 4 5 6 7 8 9 10 11 12

Orchis anatolica Boiss.
Anatolian orchid

A plant with a russet-coloured stem and grassy green leaves, dappled, and growing in a rosette. The flowers are pink to white with a large lip which has three spreading lobes. At the centre, which is light-coloured, there are two series of purple spots almost the whole length of the lip. Found in phrygana and stony locations.

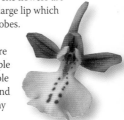

| 15-40cm ↑ |

ORCHIDACEAE

1 2 3 4 5 6 7 8 9 10 11 12

Orchis boryi Rchb. ●
Borys orchid

This orchid has the peculiarity that the upper flowers bloom first of all and thereafter the lower ones. It is dark reddish-violet or mauve in colour and the lip is light-coloured at the centre with irregular dark spots. The lip is almost semicircular, slightly divided into three lobes. The spur is of the same size as the ovary. The stem is russet-coloured at the flower-spike. Found in open meadow areas.

| 20-30cm ↑ |

ORCHIDACEAE

1 2 3 4 5 6 7 8 9 10 11 12

Orchis collina Banks & Sol.
Hill orchid

One of the first orchids to flower, this is distinguished by its undivided lip and the short, sack-like spur. The sepals are brownish-green and the lip a variety of colours from green to pink, often light-coloured at the base. It is usually found in phrygana and dry meadows.

| 10-40cm ↑ |

Orchis fragrans Pollini
Bug orchid

ORCHIDACEAE

| 1 | 2 | 3 | 4 | 5 | 6 | 7 | 8 | 9 | 10 | 11 | 12 |

The scent of this orchid is reminiscent of vanilla. It is a delicate, greenish-pink plant with a dense inflorescence. The sepals and the two petals form a sharply-peaked dome. The lip is three-lobed, the middle lobe longer, with strong red spotting at the centre. The spur is relatively short with a slight downwards inclination. Found in phrygana and meadows where there is dampness.

| 10-30cm ↑ | 🏔 ⚓

Orchis italica Poir.
Wavy-leaved monkey orchid

ORCHIDACEAE

| 1 | 2 | 3 | 4 | 5 | 6 | 7 | 8 | 9 | 10 | 11 | 12 |

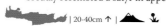

This is a widely occurring plant with a dense spike that is spherical, ovoid or pyramid-shaped, and has wavy leaves, often with dark spots. The flowers are polymorphic, pink to white with a three-lobed lip, and the middle lobe is also trilobate. The sepals and petals form a dome with the result that the whole appearance of the flower resembles that of a little man with a phallus. It was perhaps for this reason that the ancient Greeks called it 'satyrion', since it broadly resembled a satyr in appearance.

| 20-40cm ↑ | 🏔 ⚓

Orchis lactea Poir.
Milky orchid

ORCHIDACEAE

| 1 | 2 | 3 | 4 | 5 | 6 | 7 | 8 | 9 | 10 | 11 | 12 |

A beautiful orchid which has white or rose-pink flowers with pink stippling. The lip is three-lobed with the middle lobe larger, wavy at the edges, and undivided. The sepals are greenish at the base and form a closed dome together with the petals. The spur is strong, and turned downwards. Found in phrygana and grassy meadows.

| 10-20cm ↑ | 🏔 ⚓

ORCHIDACEAE

| 1 | 2 | 3 | 4 | 5 | 6 | 7 | 8 | 9 | 10 | 11 | 12 |

Orchis laxiflora Lam.
Jersey or Lax-flowered orchid

A tall plant with a loose inflorescence. The leaves are narrow and ridged. The flowers are usually a light pink, almost white at the centre. The lip is trilobate with the middle lobe smaller than the lateral lobes, the latter hanging downwards. It prefers damp localities and marshes. The same biotopes are also chosen by *O. palustris*, which is similar, but relatively larger, lighter in colour, and has horizontal lateral lobes.

| 30-60m ↑ |

ORCHIDACEAE ## *Orchis papilionacea* ssp. *alibertis* G. & H. Kretzschmar ●
Alibertis' butterfly orchid

| 1 | 2 | 3 | 4 | 5 | 6 | 7 | 8 | 9 | 10 | 11 | 12 |

This is the endemic form of *O. papilionacea* and was identified very recently. It resembles the subspecies *heroica* but is taller and has fewer, darker flowers which appear at least a month later. The leaves have already withered at the time of flowering. Found in phrygana.

| 20-40cm ↑ |

ORCHIDACEAE ## *Orchis papilionacea* ssp. *heroica* (E.D. Clarke) H. Baumann
Butterfly orchid

| 1 | 2 | 3 | 4 | 5 | 6 | 7 | 8 | 9 | 10 | 11 | 12 |

The plant has fluted, lanceolate leaves without spotting. The flowers are butterfly-shaped with sepals and petals that are darker than the lip and have deep red veining. The bracts are dark-coloured, longer than the ovary. The lip is light-coloured with pink lines and stippling, undivided, and lightly undulating at the edges. The flower-heads are relatively dense but contain few flowers. Found in phrygana and open, dry locations.

| 10-30cm ↑ |

Orchis pauciflora Ten.
Sparsely-flowering orchid

| 1 | 2 | 3 | 4 | 5 | 6 | 7 | 8 | 9 | 10 | 11 | 12 |

A relatively small plant with fluted, lanceolate leaves without stippling. The flowers are whitish-yellow, with an almost yellow lip, trilobate, irregularly toothed with dark red, irregular flecks and slight green shading at the centre. The spur is long, larger than the ovary. Found in phrygana in rocky locations.

| 10-30cm ↑ |

Orchis provincialis Balb.
Provence orchid

ORCHIDACEAE

| 1 | 2 | 3 | 4 | 5 | 6 | 7 | 8 | 9 | 10 | 11 | 12 |

This plant greatly resembles *O. pauciflora* but it is of a lighter colour, almost white. It also differs in its very individual foliage with dark flecks. The lip is three-lobed with red stippling, a hollow at the centre and lobes that are strongly turned downwards. The spur has a slight swelling at the tip. Found in phrygana, open dry locations, and in oak forests.

| 20-30cm ↑ |

Orchis quadripunctata Cirillo ex Ten.
Orchis quadripunctata

ORCHIDACEAE

| 1 | 2 | 3 | 4 | 5 | 6 | 7 | 8 | 9 | 10 | 11 | 12 |

This beautiful plant, usually short with few flowers, has a dark red stem and leaves with dark flecks. The flowers range from pink to white with outspread sepals and a very thin, long spur. The lip is three-lobed, lighter coloured at the base, and normally bears four spots, a characteristic which has given it its name. Found in stony locations.

| 5-40cm ↑ |

Orchis simia Lam.
Monkey orchid

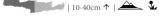

A very robust orchid, generally resembling *O. italica* with which it hybridizes. The leaves are in a rosette, and without undulations. The flower is pink, and white in the centre. The sepals and petals form a dome which looks like a head, while the central lip is three-lobed with the middle lobe bilobate with a pointed-tipped little 'tail' at the centre. The general appearance of the flower vividly recalls that of a monkey – hence the name. Relatively rare, it prefers phyrgana thickets.

| 10-40cm ↑ |

Orchis sitiaca (Renz) Delforge ●
Orchis sitiaca

This plant resembles *O. anatolica*, but differs in the very particular appearance of the silver-green leaves, which have only few or no spots, and in the much later flowering-time. The lobes of the lip are strongly turned downwards. Another particular characteristic is constituted by the green nerves on the inside of the sepals. Endemic to the mountains of Crete.

| 15-25cm ↑ |

Orchis tridentata Scop.
Three-toothed orchid

This resembles *O. lactea* but differs in that the sepals do not completely close the dome and the tips of them form three teeth, a characteristic which gives the plant its name. The lip is three-lobed with the middle lobe larger, also divided with a little protuberance at the centre. All of the tips of the lobes are pointed. Found in bushy phrygana thickets.

| 20-40cm ↑ |

Orchis prisca HAUTZ.
Cretan orchid

ORCHIDACEAE

| 1 | 2 | 3 | 4 | 5 | 6 | 7 | 8 | 9 | 10 | 11 | 12 |

This beautiful and rare orchid is endemic to Crete. It has a russet-coloured stem and lanceolate, unspeckled leaves. The flower is pink with a trilobate lip, light-coloured at the centre with dark spots. The sepals have green shading on the inside. The short, fat spur is very characteristic. The plant is found in the mountain massifs of the island.

| 10-30cm ↑ |

Serapias cordigera ssp. *cretica* B. & H. BAUMANN   ORCHIDACEAE
Heart-flowered serapias

| 1 | 2 | 3 | 4 | 5 | 6 | 7 | 8 | 9 | 10 | 11 | 12 |

The serapies do not have the impressive colouring and forms of the other orchids, since they are all more or less of the same brownish-violet colour and form. The result is that their identification is often difficult. S. cordigera is the rarest among them and has a large, reddish-pink heart-shaped lip which differentiates it. A particular characteristic is also constituted by the dark spots at the base of the stem and leaves. Found in phrygana and in low thickets.

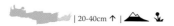

| 20-40cm ↑ |

Serapias lingua L.
Tongue serapias, tongue orchid

ORCHIDACEAE

| 1 | 2 | 3 | 4 | 5 | 6 | 7 | 8 | 9 | 10 | 11 | 12 |

This is the smallest of the serapies and easily differentiated by its tongue-like lip, a characteristic which gives the plant its name. The swellings present in other varieties at the base of the lip are absent in *S. lingua*, while another characteristic is the black fleck located there. The bracts are of the same length as the flowers which are usually of a violet or white colour. Found in phrygana, thickets, and grassy meadows, and has a preference for damp locations.

| 15-30cm ↑ |

ORCHIDACEAE **_Serapias orientalis_** (GREUTER) H. BAUMANN & KÜNKELE

| 1 | 2 | 3 | 4 | 5 | 6 | 7 | 8 | 9 | 10 | 11 | 12 |

Eastern serapias

This is a relatively small plant with a very long pointed lip which is often turned backwards. The flowers are usually concentrated in a terminal, rather compact inflorescence. The two dark lateral lobes of the lip which protrude clearly from the sheath are characteristic. Found in meadows and pine forests with a preference for damp soil.

| 20-30cm ↑ |

ORCHIDACEAE

Spiranthes spiralis KOCH.

| 1 | 2 | 3 | 4 | 5 | 6 | 7 | 8 | 9 | 10 | 11 | 12 |

Autumn Lady's Tresses

This tiny, relatively rare orchid is the only one which flowers in autumn. The leaves are concentrated in a rosette at the base of the plant and develop in spring. The inflorescence with the little white flowers has a characteristic spiral arrangement. Found in phrygana, thickets, pine forests and olive groves.

| 10-30cm ↑ |

PALMAE (ARECACEAE)

Phoenix theophrasti GREUTER ●

| 1 | 2 | 3 | 4 | 5 | 6 | 7 | 8 | 9 | 10 | 11 | 12 |

Theophrastus' palm tree

A beautiful tree, endemic to Crete, which has been classified as 'vulnerable'. It can grow to a great height and forms clumps in damp, sandy places near the sea. Male and female flowers are found on different trees, and the fruits produced are inedible. The most well-known populations of this palm are at Vai in eastern Crete and at Limni Preveli south of Rethymnon. It resembles _P. dactylifera_, which was mentioned by Theophrastus, but the fruit of the latter are edible.

| 3-15m ↑ |

A

Acantholimon androsaceum 122

Acantholimon echinus 122

Acantholimon ulicinum 122

Acanthus spinosus 21

Acer creticum 21

Acer orientalis 21

Acer sempervirens 9, 21

Aceras anthropophorum 175

Achillea cretica 46

Acinos alpinus 92

Adonis microcarpa 126

Aethionema saxatile ssp. creticum 72

Agave americana 11 151

Alcea pallida 116

Alkanna sieberi 25

Alkanna tinctoria 25

Allium ampeloprasum 16, 162

Allium callimischon ssp. haemostictum 162

Allium chamaespathum 164

Allium neapolitanum 163

Allium nigrum 163

Allium platakisii 11

Allium roseum 163

Allium rubrovittatum 164

Allium subhirsutum 164

Allium tardans 164

Alyssum fragillimum 72

Alyssum idaeum 73

Alyssum lassithicum 73

Alyssum minus 73

Alyssum saxatile 72

Alyssum simplex73

Alyssum sphacioticum73

Amelanchier ovalis ssp. cretica 131

Ammophila arenaria 157

Amygdalus webbii 132

Anacamptis pyramidalis 176

Anagallis arvensis 124

Anagallis foemina 124

Anagyris foetida 103

Anchusa aegyptiaca 26

Anchusa azurea 13, 26

Anchusa cespitosa 26

Anchusa hybrida 27

Anchusa italica 26

Anchusa undulata 27

Anchusa variegata 27

Androcymbium rechingeri 11, 165

Anemone coronaria 16, 127

Anemone hortensis ssp. heldreichii 127

Anthemis chia 47

Anthemis filicaulis 47

Anthemis glaberrima 11

Anthemis rigida 47

Anthyllis tetraphylla 103

Anthyllis vulneraria 104

Arabis alpina 73

Arbutus andrachne 80

Arbutus unedo 81

Arenaria cretica 37

Arisarum vulgare 154

Aristolochia cretica 23

Aristolochia sempervirens 24

Arum alpinum 154

Arum concinnatum 154

Arum creticum 16, 155

Arum idaeum 155

Asclepias fruticosa 24

Asparagus aphyllus 165

Asperula idaea 134

Asperula incana134

Asperula pubescens 134

Asperula rigida 135

Asphodeline liburnica 165

Asphodeline lutea 166

Asphodelus aestivus 166

Asphodelus fistulosus 166

Aster creticus 48

Aster tripolium 48

Asteriscus spinosus 61

Astracantha cretica 104

Astragalus angustifolius 104

Astragalus creticus 104

Atractylis gummifera 48

Aubrieta deltoidea 74

Aurinia saxatilis 72

B

Ballota acetabulosa 92

Ballota pseudodictamnus 92

Barlia robertiana 176

Bellardia trixago 136

Bellevalia brevipedicellata 167

Bellis longifolia 49

Bellis perennis 49

Bellis sylvestris 49

Berberis cretica 25

Biarum davisii 155

Biscutella didyma 74

Bituminaria bitominosa 111

Blackstonia perfoliata 86

Borago officinalis 27

Brassica cretica 74

Brassica nigra 75

Bryonia cretica 78

Bupleurum kakiscalae 143

C

Cakile maritima 75

Calamintha cretica 92

Calendula arvensis 50

Calicotome villosa 105

Calystegia sepium 66
Campanula aizoon 33
Campanula cretica 33
Campanula pelviformis 33
Campanula saxatilis ssp. saxatilis 34
Campanula spatulata ssp. filicaulis 14, 34
Campanula tubulosa 34
Capparis spinosa 36
Cardaria draba 75
Carlina corymbosa 50
Carlina gummifera 48
Carthamus dentatus ssp. ruber 50
Carthamus lanatus ssp. baeticus 50
Centaurea calcitrapa 51
Centaurea idaea 51
Centaurea raphanina 51
Centaurea solstitialis 14
Centaurea spinosa 52
Centaurium erythraea 86
Centaurium maritimum 87
Centaurium pulchellum 87
Centranthus calcitrapae 149
Centranthus ruber 149
Centranthus sieberii 150
Cephalanthera cucullata 176
Cerastium scaposum 38
Ceratonia siliqua 105
Cercis siliquastrum 105
Cerinthe major 28
Cerinthe retorta 28
Cerinthe retorta 28
Chionodoxa nana 9, 167
Chrysanthemum coronarium 14, 52
Chrysanthemum segetum 52
Cicer incisum 106
Cichorium intybus 53
Cichorium spinosum 53
Cionura erecta 24

Cirsium creticum ssp. creticum 53
Cirsium creticum ssp. dictaeum 53
Cirsium morinifolium 54
Cistus creticus 14, 44
Cistus incanus ssp. creticus 44
Cistus parviflorus 44
Cistus salvifolius 44
Clematis cirrhosa 127
Colchicum cretense 167
Colchicum cupani 168
Colchicum macrophyllum 16, 168
Colchicum pusillum 168
Conium maculatum 144
Convolvulus althaeoides 66
Convolvulus argyrothamnos 66
Convolvulus arvensis 67
Convolvulus dorycnium 67
Convolvulus elegantissimus 67
Convolvulus oleifolius 68
Convolvulus siculus 68
Coridothymus capitatus 102
Coronilla globosa 106
Coronilla parviflora 106
Corydalis uniflora 119
Crataegus monogyna 131
Crepis auriculifolia 54
Crepis cretica 54
Crepis neglecta ssp. cretica 54
Crepis rubra 55
Crepis sibthorpiana 55
Crepis tybakiensis 54
Crithmum maritimum 149
Crocus boryi 157
Crocus cartwrightianus 157
Crocus laevigatus 158
Crocus oreocreticus 9, 158
Crocus sieberi ssp. sieberi 158
Crocus tournefortii 159
Crupina crupinastrum 55
Cupressus sempervirens var.

horizontalis 9, 20
Cuscuta atrans 68
Cyclamen creticum 124
Cyclamen graecum 16, 124
Cyclamen hederifolium 125
Cynoglossum columnae 28
Cynoglossum creticum 28
Cynoglossum sphacioticum 29
Cytinus hypocistis 126

D

Dactylorhiza romana 177
Daphne gnidioides 141
Daphne oleoides 142
Daphne sericea 142
Datura stramonium 140
Daucus carota 144
Delphinium staphisagria 128
Dianthus juniperinus 38
Dianthus sphacioticus 38
Dittrichia graveolens 56
Dittrichia viscosa 56
Dracunculus vulgaris 156
Drimia maritima 175

E

Ebenus cretica 107
Ecballium elaterium 79
Echinops spinosissimus 56
Echium angustifolium 29
Echium italicum 29
Echium plantagineum 30
Epipactis cretica 177
Epipactis microphylla 177
Erica arborea 81
Erica manipuliflora 81
Erigeron glabratus 57
Erodium gruinum 87
Eryngium campestre 144
Eryngium creticum 145
Eryngium maritimum 145
Erysimum candicum ssp. candicum 76

Erysimum creticum 76
Erysimum mutabile 76
Erysimum raulinii 77
Euphorbia acanthothamnos 82
Euphorbia characias 15, 82
Euphorbia dendroides 82
Euphorbia helioscopia 83
Euphorbia herniariifolia 83
Euphorbia paralias 83
Euphorbia peplis 84
Euphorbia rechingeri 84

F

Ferula commmunis 145
Ferulago nodosa 146
Ficus carica 117
Fritillaria graeca 18
Fritillaria messanensis 168
Fumana arabica 45
Fumana paphlagonica ssp.
alpina 45
Fumana thymifolia 45
Fumaria capreolata 119
Fumaria officinalis 119

G

Gagea bohemica 169
Gagea graeca 169
Gagea peduncularis 169
Galactites tomentosa 57
Genista acanthoclada107
Geranium robertianum 88
Geranium tuberosum 88
Geropogon hybridus 65
Gladiolus italicus 159
Glaucium flavum 120
Globularia alypum 88
Gomphocarpus fruticosus 24
Gynandriris monophylla 159
Gynandriris sisyrinchium
16, 160

H

Hedera helix 23
Helianthemum hymettium 46
Helichrysum barrelieri 58
Helichrysum doerfleri 11, 57
Helichrysum heldreichii 58
Helichrysum italicum 58
Helichrysum microphyllum 58
Helichrysum stoechas 58
Heliotropium europaeum 30
Hermodactylus tuberosus 160
Himatoglossum samariense 177
Hyoscyamus albus 140
Hypericum amblycalyx 89
Hypericum empetrifolium ssp.
empetrifolium 89
Hypericum empetrifolium ssp.
oliganthum 89
Hypericum empetrifolium ssp.
tortuosum 90
Hypericum jovis 89
Hypericum kelleri 90
Hypericum perfoliatum 90
Hypericum perforatum 15, 91
Hypericum trichocaulon 91
Hypericum triquetrifolium 91

I

Inula crithmoides 59
Inula graveolens 56
Inula viscosa 56
Iris cretensis 160
Iris germanica 161
Iris pseudacorus 161
Iris unguicularis
ssp. cretensis 160

J

Juniperus oxycedrus 20
Juniperus phoenicea 20

K

Knautia integrifolia 79

L

Lamium amplexicaule 93
Lamium garganicum 93
Lamyropsis cynaroides 59
Lathyrus clymenum107
Laurentia gasparini 36
Laurus nobilis 103
Lavandula stoechas 93
Lavatera bryonifolia 116
Lavatera cretica 116
Lecokia cretica 146
Legousia falcata 35
Legousia pentagonia 35
Legousia speculum-veneris 35
Lepidium draba 75
Limodorum abortivum 178
Limonium creticum 122
Limonium sinuatum 122
Linum arboreum114
Linum bienne 115
Lithodora hispidula 30
Lithospermum incrassatum 31
Lomelosia brachiata 80
Lomelosia sphaciotica 80
Lonicera etrusca 37
Lotus cytisoides 108
Lupinus albus 108
Lupinus angustifolius 108
Lupinus pilosus 109
Lysimachia serpyllifolia 125
Lythrum junceum 115

M

Malcomia flexuosa 77
Malva cretica 117
Malva sylvestris 117
Mandragora autumnalis 140
Mandragora officinarum 140
Matthiola sinuata 14, 77
Matthiola tricuspidata 78
Mattiastrum
lithospermifolium 31

Medicago arborea 109
Medicago marina 109
Medicago strasseri 110
Mentha pulegium 94
Minuartia verna 39
Muscari commutatum 169
Muscari comosum 170
Muscari neglectum 170
Muscari spreitzenhoferi 170
Myrtus communis 118

N

Narcissus serotinus 152
Narcissus tazetta 16, 152
Neotinea maculata 178
Nepeta hirsuta 94
Nepeta melissifolia 94
Nepeta scordotis 94
Nerium oleander 22
Nicotiana glauca 141
Nigella damascena 128
Notobasis syriaca 59

O

Oenanthe pimpinelloides 146
Onobrychis sphaciotica 110
Ononis reclinata 110
Ononis spinosa 111
Onopordum bracteatum ssp. creticum 60
Onopordum illyricum 60
Onopordum tauricum 60
Onosma erectum 31
Onosma graecum 32
Ophrys apifera 178
Ophrys ariadnae 179
Ophrys basilissa 179
Ophrys bombyliflora 179
Ophrys candica 180
Ophrys creberrima 180
Ophrys cressa 180
Ophrys cretica 181
Ophrys cretica ssp. ariadnae 179
Ophrys creticola 181
Ophrys episcopalis 181
Ophrys fleischmannii 182
Ophrys fusca ssp. creberrima 180
Ophrys fusca ssp. cressa 180
Ophrys fusca ssp. creticola 181
Ophrys fusca ssp. thriptiensis 186
Ophrys gortynia 185
Ophrys gregoriana 182
Ophrys heldreichii 182
Ophrys herae 183
Ophrys iricolor 183
Ophrys mammosa 183
Ophrys mesaritica 184
Ophrys omegaifera 184
Ophrys phryganae 184
Ophrys sicula 185
Ophrys sitiaca 185
Ophrys sphaciotica 182
Ophrys sphegodes ssp. gortynia 185
Ophrys sphegodes ssp. cretensis 185
Ophrys spruneri 186
Ophrys spruneri ssp. gregoriana 182
Ophrys tenthredinifera 186
Ophrys thriptiensis 186
Opopanax hispidus 147
Opuntia ficus-indica 32
Orchis anatolica 187
Orchis boryi 187
Orchis collina 187
Orchis fragrans 188
Orchis italica 188
Orchis lactea 188
Orchis laxiflora 189
Orchis palustris 189
Orchis papilionacea ssp. alibertis 189
Orchis papilionacea ssp. heroica 189
Orchis pauciflora 190
Orchis prisca 192
Orchis provincialis 190
Orchis quadripunctata 190
Orchis simia 191
Orchis sitiaca 191
Orchis tridentata 191
Origanum dictamnus 95
Origanum microphyllum 95
Origanum onites 95
Origanum vulgare 95
Orlaya grandiflora 147
Ornithogalum creticum 171
Ornithogalum dictaeum ssp. dictaeum 171
Ornithogalum exscapum 171
Ornithogalum narbonense 172
Ornithogalum nutans 18, 172
Ornithogalum pyramidale 172
Ornithogalum sibthorpii 172
Otanthus maritimus 61
Oxalis pes-caprae 118

P

Paeonia clusii 7, 118
Pallenis spinosa 61
Pancratium maritimum 11, 152
Papaver apulum 120
Papaver argemone ssp. nigrotinctum 120
Papaver purpureomarginatum 120
Papaver rhoeas 121
Papaver somniferum 14
Paracaryum lithospermifolium 31
Parentucellia latifolia 136
Parentucellia viscosa 137
Paronychia macrosepala 39
Petromarula pinnata 36
Petrorhagia candica 39
Petrorhagia dianthoides 39

Petrorhagia velutina 40
Phagnalon graecum 61
Phagnalon pumilum 62
Phagnalon pygmaeum 62
Phlomis cretica 96
Phlomis fruticosa 96
Phlomis lanata 96
Phoenix theophrasti 11, 193
Phytolacca americana 121
Picnomon acarna 62
Pimpinella tragium subsp.
depressa 147
Pinus brutia 9, 21
Pistacia lentiscus 22
Pistacia terebinthus 22
Platanus orientalis 121
Polygala venulosa 123
Polygonum idaeum 123
Portulaca oleracea 123
Prasium majus 97
Primula vulgaris 125
Procopiania cretica 32
Prunella cretensis 97
Prunella laciniata 97
Prunus prostrata 132
Prunus webbii 132
Psoralea bituminosa 111
Pterocephalus papposus 79
Ptilostemon chamaepeuce 62
Punica granatum 126
Putoria calabrica 135

Q

Quercus coccifera 9, 85
Quercus ilex 85
Quercus macrolepis 85
Quercus pubescens 86

R

Ranunculus asiaticus 16, 128
Ranunculus bullatus 129
Ranunculus creticus 129
Ranunculus cupreus 129

Ranunculus ficaria 130
Reseda alba 130
Reseda lutea 130
Reseda luteola 131
Ricinus communis 84
Romulea bulbocodium 161
Romulea linaresii
ssp. graeca 162
Rosa canina 132
Rosa corymbifera 132
Rosa glutinosa 133
Rosa pulverulenta 133
Rosa sempervirens 133
Rosmarinus officinalis 97
Rosularia serrata 69
Rubus sanctus 133
Rubus ulmifolius 133
Ruscus aculeatus 172
Ruta chalepensis 135

S

Salsola kali 43
Salsola soda 43
Salvia fruticosa 98
Salvia pomifera 98
Salvia triloba 98
Salvia verbenaca 98
Salvia viridis 99
Sambucus ebulus 37
Sarcopoterium spinosum 134
Satureja spinosa 99
Satureja thymbra 99
Saxifraga chrysosplenifolia 136
Scabiosa atropurpurea 79
Scabiosa maritima 79
Scabiosa sphaciotica 80
Scabioza minoana ssp.
asterusica 10
Scilla autumnalis 173
Scilla nana 167
Scolymus hispanicus 63
Scorzonera cretica 63
Scrophularia heterophylla 137

Scrophularia lucida 137
Scrophularia peregrina 138
Scutellaria hirta 100
Scutellaria sieberi 100
Securigera globosa 106
Securigera parviflora 106
Sedum album 69
Sedum amplexicaule 69
Sedum creticum 70
Sedum laconicum 70
Sedum littoreum 70
Sedum praesidis 70
Sedum rubens 71
Senecio fruticulosus 63
Senecio rupestris 64
Serapias cordigera
ssp. cretica 192
Serapias lingua 192
Serapias orientalis 193
Sesleria doerfleri 156
Sideritis syriaca
ssp. syriaca 100
Silene antri jovis 9
Silene behen 40
Silene bellidifolia 40
Silene colorata 41
Silene cretica 14, 41
Silene dichotoma 41
Silene gallica 42
Silene sedoides 42
Silene succulenta 42
Silene variegata 43
Silene vulgaris 43
Silybum marianum 64
Sinapis alba 78
Sixalix atropurpurea 79
Smilax aspera 173
Smyrnium olusatrum 148
Smyrnium rotundifolium 148
Solenopsis minuta 36
Spartium junceum 111
Spiranthes spiralis 193
Stachys cretica 15, 101

Stachys spinosa 101
Staehelina arborea 64
Staehelina fruticosa 65
Staehelina petiolata 64
Sternbergia greuteriana 153
Sternbergia lutea 153
Sternbergia sicula 153
Styrax officinalis 141
Symphyamdra cretica 33

T

Tamus communis 156
Tetragonolobus purpureus 112
Teucrium alpestre 101
Teucrium divaricatum 102
Teucrium graecum 102
Thymelaea hirsuta 142
Thymelaea tartonraira 143
Thymus capitatus 102
Thymus leucotrichus 102
Tordylium apulum 148
Tragopogon hybridus 65
Tragopogon porrifolius 65
Tragopogon sinuatus 65
Tremastelma palaestinum 80
Trifolium campestre 112
Trifolium repens 112
Trifolium stellatum 113
Trifolium uniflorum 113
Trigonella balansae 113
Tripodion tetraphyllum 103
Tuberaria guttata 46
Tulipa bakeri 7, 18, 173
Tulipa cretica 174
Tulipa doerfleri 174
Tulipa goulimyi 174
Tulipa saxatilis 175

U

Umbilicus horizontalis 71
Umbilicus parviflorus 71
Umbilicus rupestris 71
Urginea maritima 175

V

Valeriana asarifolia 150
Verbascum arcturus 138
Verbascum macrurum 138
Verbascum sinuatum 139
Verbascum spinosum 139
Veronica thymifolia 139
Vicia cretica 114
Vicia tenuifolia 114
Vicia villosa 114
Vinca major 23
Viola fragrans 151
Viola scorpiuroides 151
Viscum album 115
Vitex agnus castus 150

Z

Zelkova abelicea 143
Zelkova cretica 143

BIBLIOGRAPHY

Α. Άλκιμος, *Οι ορχιδέες της Ελλάδας*, Αθήνα 1988

Θ. Αραμπατζή, *Αγριολούλουδα του παρθένου δάσους Δράμας*, Δράμα 1997

Θ. Αραμπατζή, *Θάμνοι και δέντρα στην Ελλάδα*, Δράμα 2001

Ε. Βάθης, *Τα φυτά του πάρκου της Αρχαίας Αγοράς*, Αθήνα 2002

M. Blamey, C. Grey-Wilson, W*ild Flowers of the Mediterranean*

D. Burnie, *Wildflowers of the Mediterranean*

Π. Γενναδίου, *Φυτολογικό Λεξικό*, Αθήναι 1914

J. Fielding and N. Turland, Flowers of Crete, Kew 2005

N. Goulandris, C. Goulimis, *Wild Flowers of Greece*, Athens 1968

A. Huxley, *Flowers in Greece, an outline of the flora*, London 1972

R. Jahn, P. Schönfelder, *Excursionsflora für Kreta*, Stuttgart 1995

Δ. Καββαδα, *Εικονογραφημένον Βοτανικόν-Φυτολογικόν Λεξικόν*, Αθήναι

H. & G. Kretzschmar, W Eccarius, *Ορχιδέες, Κρήτη και Δωδεκάνησα*, Ρέθυμνο 2004

Έ. Μπάουμαν, *Η Ελληνική χλωρίδα στο μύθο, στην τέχνη στη λογοτεχνία*, Αθήνα 1984

Β. Παπιομύτογλου, *Σαμαριά, το Φαράγγι και τα Λευκά Όρη* , Ρέθυμνο 2006

O. Polunin, A. Huxley, *Flowers of the Mediterranean*, London 1987

O. Polunin, *Flowers of Greece and the Balkans*, Oxford 1987

A. Strid, *Mountain flora of Greece*, Vol. 1, Cambridge 1986

A. Strid, Kit Tan, *Mountain flora of Greece*, Vol. 2, Edinburg 1991

A. Strid, *Wild flowers of mount Olympus*, Αθήνα 1980

Γ. Σφήκα, *Αγριολούλουδα της Ελλάδας*, Αθήνα

Γ. Σφήκα, *Αγριολούλουδα της Κρήτης*, Αθήνα

Γ. Σφήκα, *Οι βοτανικοί παράδεισοι της Ελλάδας*, Αθήνα 2001

Kit Tan, G. Iatrou, *Endemic plants of Greece, the Peloponnese*, Copenhagen 2001

The Red Data Book of Rare and Threatened plants of Greece, 1995

N. J. Turland, L. Chilton, J. R. Press *Flora of the Cretan area*, London 1993

J. Zaffran, *Contributions a la flore et a la vegetation de la Crete*, Aix en Provence 1990